TEN FIGHTER BC

TEN FIGHTER BOYS

Edited by

Wing-Commander ATHOL FORBES, D.F.C.

and

Squadron-Leader HUBERT ALLEN, D.F.C.

Collins

Collins
A division of HarperCollins Publishers
77-85 Fulham Palace Road
London W6 8JB
www.collins.co.uk

First published by Collins in 1942

1 3 5 7 9 10 8 6 4 2

A catalogue record for this book is available from the British Library

ISBN 978-0-00-723693-0

Designed and typeset by MATS, Southend-on-Sea, Essex
Printed and bound in Great Britain by Clay Ltd, St Ives plc

To the Memory of PETER STUDD, KEN GILLIES, GEORGE CORBETT, Sgt. SMITH, JOHNNY MATHER, MAXY MAXWELL, BUTCH BAKER, MOULDY MILDREN, PETER KING, Flight-Sergeant HAYMAN, Sgt. Rob TAYLOR, Sgt. GREEN, Sgt. CLAUDE PARSONS, TED HOGG, PICKLE PICKERING, and BOGLE BODIE, all of the old squadron, who lost their lives as they would have wished, flying SPITFIRES in defence of their country, is this book very humbly dedicated.

THE TEN FIGHTER BOYS

Doug Hunt

John 'Durex' Kendal

Jimmy 'Binder' Corbin

Crelin 'Bogle' Bodie

Robert 'Oxo' Oxspring

Max Maxwell

Hubert 'Dizzy' Allen

Athol Forbes

John 'Pickle' Pickering

Claude Parsons

CONTENTS

LIST OF ILLUSTRATIONS

FOREWORD

It was November 1940 and I and the other pilots of 66 Squadron were sheltering from the cold in the dispersal hut at Biggin Hill aerodrome, each of us glad to be back from another sortie. The conversation flowed back and forth, very little of it serious, then Sqn Ldr Athol Forbes joined us. He had aspirations of becoming a writer after the war. He thought it would be a good idea if we pilots wrote the stories of our experience while our memories were fresh from the heat of battle. He would edit them and have them printed and published. We eventually got round to this in early 1941 and ten of us handed our stories to Sqn Ldr Forbes. The result was the book *Ten Fighter Boys* published in 1942 by Collins.

The pilots were a mixed bunch from many walks of life and various experience as combat pilots – NCOs and officers. It is sad to say that some of the pilots were killed before the book was published.

My particular effort was written in about March 1941 when I was 23½ years old, the second oldest in the squadron at that time. It was always hard when we lost pilots but we could not afford to dwell on these occasions. We had a job to do and dying was a very possible part of the job. We all did our best and now I do my best to remember the good times and not the bad.

I was surprised and delighted when I was informed that Collins were re-issuing the book after all these years, over

66 years. It will be a very fitting tribute to my old colleagues of 66 Squadron, all of them no longer with us. It will also be great for any of their families and friends. They were a fantastic bunch of young men, all characters in their own way, good fun to be with and we always had a very strong sense of trust. I am proud and very grateful to have had the privilege of knowing them.

Looking back I think I really enjoyed my flying time especially in such a beautiful aeroplane, the magnificent Spitfire. It was an extraordinary time to have lived through, the fantastic sense of comradeship, and the trust between us kept us going through the many days often fraught with danger. We had our moments of triumph and of course fear and I was one of the lucky few to survive to tell the tale. I must finally add that the publishing of my book *Last of the Ten Fighter Boys* has brought me refreshed interest and many new friends. It was amazing that during my signing sessions a number of people turned up with a copy of *Ten Fighter Boys* for me to sign – an indication of how the book has been cherished over the years. Now it will be available for a new audience.

Jimmy Corbin

INTRODUCTION

THE IDEA occurred to me one morning over a cup of coffee. My squadron had just returned from a sortie involving a spot of bother with a large number of Huns, and we pilot boys were taking it easy. General conversation was going on about what was to be done when the war had finished and there were no vacuum cleaners to be sold. Someone or other had decided to take a dozen battle-scarred Spitfires over to America complete with war veteran pilots to give displays of aerobatics and fake combat over various parts of the States.

I remember thinking it a good idea. Then the idea of this book sprang to life. I had always been interested in journalism, and for some unknown reason thought that I would be some use at the game. I knew that after the last war thousands of books had been published on life in the trenches, aerial combat, naval actions, etc. But why wait until after the war? People would be so much more enthralled to read first-hand about events that were going on all round at the time of reading. Even more so if the book was written jointly by a few of "the few" who were still living through all these immense happenings.

And we got to work. We began in November, 1940, and here, after many months of trial and error, is the result, by ten pilots, most of whom have seen action in the Battle of Britain, and later, in the Battle of France.

Three of the original authors are now dead – killed in

action. A number of other pilots started to write about their flying experiences with us, but they were killed before their work had assumed sufficient proportions for inclusion in the book. But of the ten pilots whose work you are about to read, seven are still alive at the time of writing. God only knows how many will see the war through.

The original idea was that all the pilots in the squadron should write a few thousand words about their experiences in flying and combat. Each pilot would in this way write a complete chapter of the book.

No effort has been made to alter the phraseology. What you are about to read is as pilots would and did express themselves. The language is not always drawing-room. One doesn't think in terms of drawing-rooms when one is 30,000 feet above the earth, turning and twisting to avoid a hail of lead and explosives. Raw, primitive, the instinct of self-preservation always to the foreground – that is how one's mind works under those conditions, and in that manner this book is written.

I will give you a brief outline of the squadron concerned, and then of the pilots who are mentioned in the book.

The squadron was formed in the last war, and after disbandment re-formed in 1936. It was the original Spitfire Squadron, and carried out all the necessary squadron tests on that most loved of all aircraft.

The outbreak of war found it in East Anglia, and it moved nearer the coast just before Dunkirk. It fought over Rotterdam, The Hague, Dunkirk, and moved into the front line of London at the end of August, 1940.

Since then, it has done its quota over the Atlantic, over

the North Sea, France, Belgium and Holland. I think it's the best squadron in the Air Force, but then I'm prejudiced.

The members of the squadron were a truly motley throng, consisting of young men from every walk of life. Regular Air Force officers, sergeant-pilots who had, in peace-time, been dockhands, clerks, motor-mechanics; there was even an ex-dirt-track motor-cycle expert with us. Every conceivable type was represented.

I will now introduce you to the lads who wrote the book. Bob is a tallish, good-looking, fair-headed bloke, with a typical schoolboy complexion, liable to blush every now and then. He joined the squadron at the time when it was re-equipping with Spitfires. He can take his beer like a man, comes from the North and has a very typical Yorkshire outlook. A little shy, he may appear off-hand at first, but having broken down his barriers of reserve, you would find a lovable, gay, carefree youth of twenty-two years. He won his D.F.C. in October, 1940, for shooting down Huns. His father, funnily enough, served in the same squadron in the last war and won the M.C. and bar. We all hope that Bob will also get his bar.

Dizzy is a different kettle of fish who took longer to get his D.F.C., as might be expected from his character. Medium stocky build, he likes to call the colour of his hair titian or auburn – actually it's red. He has just a touch of the old school-tie about him. He behaves as his name implies, being the life and soul of the party in his more convivial moments. In the air he is very cautious, and always behind before looking ahead.

He was most annoyed when someone cut his tail off one

day and he had to bale-out. The air around his parachute was blue, but on receiving a very liberal amount of whisky at the local where he conveniently landed, his feelings were somewhat modified.

Bogle was a real character. Imagine a particularly husky "dead-end kid," and you have Bogle. Being a strong individualist he is decidedly unconventional in appearance, usually wearing a uniform which, to say the least of it, would not pass muster on a ceremonial parade, with a colourful scarf round his neck and a large sheath-knife in his boot.

His language is foul, but he possesses more character than any one I can remember. Honest as the day, he is absolutely straight, and he never did any one a bad turn – with the possible exception of a number of Huns. He very soon got his D.F.C., and appears to prefer flying on his back to the right way up. A truly magnificent pilot.

Durex is young and noisy. The clown of the squadron, he can imitate every noise conceivable, from an underground train pulling out of a station to the ricochetting of a rifle bullet. Something had to happen before he would shut up – a little Durex went a long way. On his first operational sortie he shot down an ME. 109; on each of his next three sorties he was shot up himself.

Pickle is a funny little fellow. He's thin and long-legged and looks half-starved, but he eats more than any one else in the squadron. His hair is all over the place; I don't think even glue would keep it down, especially that funny little tuft slap in the middle. An amateur runner in peace-time, he walks twice as fast as any one else and leans forward as if he were pushing against a head-wind. You'd never think he could run a yard without breaking his legs, but if you try to catch him you'll soon find out your mistake. He is completely hare-brained; talks fast and incoherently. In an aeroplane he flies faster and lower than any one I know. If Pickle is beating you up, you have to be on your belly to avoid him.

Half a pint of beer and Pickle is "well away"; a pint, and he goes to sleep in a corner.

Max was with us all too short a time before he was killed in a Channel dog-fight. He was a tremendously strong youth and an amateur boxer – a good fellow to have in a rough-house – and tougher than they make most of us. Shy, diffident, he had a good brain. When he just did not come back we felt his loss keenly.

Duggie was a flight-sergeant and had done a hell of a lot of flying. He was shot down, and baled out over Dunkirk, but he managed to get back in a boat. He has a very droll manner and a terrific scheme about a revolution after the war, so that the whole of the country can be governed by pilots – perhaps it is not such a bad idea either.

Parsons is now, alas, missing, believed killed over Holland. A first-class man, he realised a long ambition when he flew his first Spitfire, as he had been helping to make them at Vickers' for many years before the war. Short and tubby, he was a little old at twenty-six to be a fighter-pilot, but he was just up for a D.F.M. when he was lost.

Binder Corbin finishes the list. Always moaning – usually about leave – he was the image of George Formby except that he was born in Kent and proud of it.

Thee average age of those boys was twenty-one years. At twenty-one they had seen more of Heaven and Earth –

especially Heaven – than most people dream of at sixty.

A funny thing about our game is the suddenness with which things happen. I remember once going on patrol when I hadn't seen a Hun for about four months, and then, incidentally, I only saw that one after my aeroplane had been hit by forty of his bullets, one of which went through my starboard arm. I had as my number two a raw sergeant-pilot, full of dash, absolutely fearless and with no idea about how to shoot down Huns. We were stooging along sixty miles out to sea after a so-called enemy aircraft, when I suddenly saw a few spots in the distance. On closer examination, they proved to be three Heinkels escorted by half a dozen ME.s. My first instinct was to bolt, but I went on. After a hell of a scrap, we got two ME. 109's and the rest of the party retired in disorder.

That occurred after a lull of some months, and it was, incidentally, the only action fought around our coasts on that day. I had no idea when I took off that there was anything doing or that I would so much as smell a Hun. It's just the luck of the game.

Another thing about fighting that the land-lubber may not appreciate is the business of windscreens and hoods getting frozen over. At altitude, hoar-frost always appears on the cockpit hoods owing to the intense cold, and whenever we have to lose height rapidly, the inside of the windscreen becomes covered in ice. It's impossible to see forward or upwards under these conditions and it's mighty unpleasant, for as fast as you wipe the stuff off, it ices up again. Once I had taken a dive at a Hun, a JU. 87 it was, and my windscreen iced up. I couldn't sight him through the windscreen so I had to make a rough guess through the perspex at the side of the windscreen. Funnily enough he blew up, but I expect that many a good Nazi has got away with his life because the other fellow couldn't see him on account of ice.

I wonder if any non-flying people realise the importance of keen sight in this fighting racket? Very few, I expect. Pickle had extraordinarily good sight, and he would sometimes say that there were some Huns above us which I could not see until I'd gazed up for about five minutes. The Poles usually have exceptionally good eyesight, as have most of our fighter-aces. After all, you can't shoot an aeroplane down until you see it, and with three dimensions to look around in there's quite a bit of sky which needs to be scanned.

Another bit of inside information is the never-ending argument which wages between pilots who like aerobatics and those who don't. The former school of thought – to which your humble servant subscribes – maintains that aerobatics are good for the soul and are completely essential to a successful fighter-pilot. The latter – sometimes called dead-beat school – will assure you that aerobatics are bad for the aeroplanes, and for the instruments, and are completely non-essential in the shooting down of a Hun. They may be perfectly correct, but we (and by we I speak for the school of aerobatic thought) consider that a man cannot be master of his aeroplane until he has done everything humanly possible with it. And further, that until a man is complete master of his aeroplane, he has no right to charge about the sky, as he constitutes a menace to friend and foe alike. We agree that a dog-fight with a Hun very rarely entails a considered aerobatic movement as an evasive action. In fact, the more ham-fisted the movement, the better its effect.

I have often seen aircraft firing whilst on their backs when in the middle of an almighty scrap, and I'm sure that it is not possible to sight accurately whilst on your back unless you have practised flying in this manner time and time again. I remember an ME. 109 giving me what I presumed to be an unintentional aerobatic display one fine day in 1940. It happened that I heard the rattle of guns behind me and took very violent evasive action. As I did so, an ME. 109 flashed past me, pulled up in front, and performed a complete flick roll before shooting earthwards. What he had obviously intended to do on overshooting me was to flick over and spin down, but being a little ham, he overdid the manœuvre and came out the right way up. I was so enthralled by the picture that I forgot to fire until he was on his way earthwards.

When trying to recall to memory events of this nature, it's surprising how the little things stand out in the mind. The ME. I was just telling you about had a huge red nose, and to this day, if I close my eyes and think about the action, I can distinctly see in my mind's eye that red nose flashing past me.

Another funny thing about combat is the vague and jumbled picture that one gets immediately afterwards. I can only remember having seen the black crosses on a German machine on two occasions. I think one knows instinctively when an aeroplane is hostile. On one occasion I had beaten up a 109, and his engine was stopped. I yelled out jubilantly over the Radio Telephony, "I've just got a 109." Yet on landing, the only clear recollection I had of the action was of seeing the other fellow's parachute going down.

I expect most people wonder what it must be like to have to bale-out. I used to wonder also, until one day when I had a collision in the air. I didn't know the full extent of the damage to my aeroplane, all I knew was that I'd got no airscrew, and the other fellow's tail-plane had knocked my windscreen off. I was at 6,000 feet, which isn't too high, and I had to make a horrible decision – to bale-out or try and force-land. The latter would entail the risk of the aircraft falling to pieces on me, whilst I didn't like to think of the former. The thing which decided me was the fact that I'd instinctively loosened all my straps and tubes and I couldn't risk a crash-landing unless I was tightly strapped in. So over the side I went, with my hand on the rip-cord. I honestly don't remember falling or pulling the rip-cord, or even letting it go, but my next impression is one of a deathly silence and a huge canopy above me. I seemed to be stationary 'twixt Heaven and Earth. I finally landed up a tree, hanging twenty feet from the ground. When I scrambled down the trunk, the Home Guard were all for shooting me. I managed to convince them of my identity, however, before they took that step, and went to a nearby house where I was treated to a distinctly large whisky with a touch of soda.

What glorious days those were: blue English skies, with always the chance of seeing a Hun. Knowing that your country depended on you, that every one's prayers and hopes were with you; the excitement of the chase; the exhilaration of seeing your opponent going down in flames, whilst at the same time knowing that your chances were equal. The trip home at unprecedented speeds; your base; the final beat-up with the inevitable upward Charlie or victory roll. And then your fitter's jubilance at your success; a cup of steaming-hot tea, and after that, who knows?

On that note I will leave you to read the true stories of a few fighter-pilots.

H.A.

INTRODUCING DUGGIE

Duggie is of medium height, stocky build, dark and very quiet until you get him on a party; the type of bloke that never asks fool questions and thinks well before he answers. He has a peculiar short, nervous laugh, a grand sense of humour and a wonderful knack of enjoying every minute of life. He has an enormous beer-drinking capacity and once dumbfounded the petty-officers of a well-known destroyer by drinking all except one of them under the table.

He was the senior sergeant-pilot and one of the most important blokes in the squadron, a first-class peelow and very definite capabilities as an organiser and administrator.

I hope that shortly he will get his commission, and that we will be able to retain him in the squadron. I also look forward to the day when he will become a flight-commander, a job which I know he will do exceptionally well.

Duggie's Story

THE curtain goes up at the end of May when "Peacekrieg" became "Blitzkrieg" with a vengeance. Apart from two "shows" at the time of Rotterdam's fall, the squadron had seen practically no action. Following these "do's" we made two moves in quick succession, remaining at one aerodrome for little over a week. Having barely landed and refuelled after our last shift, one of the flight-commanders went about rounding up the majority of sergeant-pilots, telling them in hushed tones that we were going places, and advising us to get small kit packed up in ten minutes, ready to fly again. During that ten minutes we rushed to our quarters in the mess, some of us grumbling about the lack of warning and all the messing around we'd suffered during the past fortnight. A plaintive murmur in colonial English from "Digger" – "I shan't be able to write to me wife" – and we all burst out laughing, since every day regularly, this newly-wed had told his Doris of his love and other sweet nothings. After delving into kit which had just arrived, and swearing "not by Kolynos," I managed to sort out the necessary. It's funny, but when you are told of an impending offensive action, you all get so keyed-up with the future trip as the predominant subject of your grey matter, even to the extent of becoming forgetful about the ordinary things of life. It wouldn't surprise me at all to see someone who is turfed out of bed for a sweep at short notice, clamber into his aircraft in pyjamas, having forgotten all about the minor detail of a pair of slacks.

So a quarter of an hour later saw 14 Spitfires take the air with the occupants loaded-up to the eyebrows and resembling the proverbial Xmas tree. Myself, in the restricted space to spare, had crammed a respirator, shaving tackle and all necessities for "bed and board." If feelings were any criterion I emulated the prince of poultry and felt completely stuffed.

Only one or two pilots besides our C.O. knew the destination, and I'm afraid my formation flying left quite a lot to be desired, as I tried to keep position on my leader with one eye whilst trying to survey the ground below with the other. We were going west, that was certain; then after 40 minutes or so a very large town with balloons easily seen against the sun. Ah, Birmingham, I thought – but what were we doing passing the Midlands like this – were we *en route* for Ireland? Had the Führer sprung another surprise? Eventually after much speculation (all wrong) we touched down on the runways on a Home Counties aerodrome – "K." We quickly refuelled and pushed on to another one – "G," some 10 minutes distant. During the brief spell at "K," I looked it over with what might be called a "pilot's eye." That is, trees and stately buildings which appear as beautifiers, read through a pilot's eyes as a nuisance and the possible cause of a crash on landing. I well remember Paddy saying what a sod it would be for night-flying here. And those balloons! God, the chaps here *must* be good, flying day in and day out so close to these pilots' dreads.

At "G" I saw more Spitfires than I had hitherto imagined possible to park on one field. Truly Britain's might in the skies, little dreaming of the future hades to come. After a "confab," it was passed around that we were to sweep the Dunkirk area as a protection for the evacuation. Our squadron were chosen to be top dogs above three others, and had to be content to waffle along at about 26,000 feet. "Oh Christ," was said a dozen times if it was said once. I myself was one offender when the valve on the oxygen bottle would only turn with the greatest of difficulty. These things normally don't worry me much, but the tense state of mind led to far less patience with the things which weren't "just so."

At last with a thunderous roar we all took off and sorted out our respective positions. I saw nothing of the other three squadrons after we approached the English coast, being busy keeping station and sharp look-out. In fact to be precise, I saw nothing of anything the whole trip. A completely uneventful trip apart from a bloody chilly feeling where my feet ought to have been. After a slight miscalculation by the C.O. we pancaked back on the runways at "K." The squadron-leader had had us quite perturbed for a quarter of an hour, during which time we looked over the side to see only sea, and plenty of it, and a low fuel-gauge reading didn't exactly promote a contented frame of mind. It was damn funny really, on reflection, to see the whole squadron open out on crossing the English coast, in failing light and poor visibility, every one trying to be the first in establishing our position and sighting our base. The trip cost us one aeroplane when the undercart failed to come down on one chap's "kyte," resulting in a sensational tearing noise as terra firma grabbed at his fuselage. There was one other "ring-twitch" effort when a sergeant-pilot, "Jock," landed across the runway and looked all the way as though he had an urgent date with a scrap heap. Anyway, hard application of brakes to the tune of sergeant-major's rhetoric averted another calamity.

That night we were very thankful to two W.A.A.F. N.C.O.s who, although they weren't cooks (at least according to R.A.F. documents), turned out a lovely set of cooked suppers for the sergeant-pilots, an event which I shan't forget quickly.

The next morning we had an early "stand-to" period, when another invasion rumour seemed to grip every one, then after breakfast we shoved-off to our marshalling base at "G" again. Here was a repetition of yesterday's landscape except that another squadron had tootled in to swell the band of happy pilgrims.

We did two sweeps over Dunkirk that day, at least the squadron did, as I had to stand down on the first one to let our spare men have a crack. These two sweeps were replicas of the first with yours-truly doing "tail-end Charlie" at 25,000 feet or over, not seeing anything, and learning afterwards that one or two of the lower boys had a few sharp tussles. I suppose, though, we served our purpose in protecting the mob from attack from above. Most of the officers and sergeants saw no reason why on the next trip we shouldn't be one of the lower squadrons and let someone else have a go at the synthetic ozone. At least, I thought the lower temperature would make us more comfortable. We all had a moan to the C.A. about it, and he in turn was in full agreement.

That evening we returned to our parent station at "D," much to every one's delight, for it was here that the squadron was born and brought up, right to the time of opening this narrative. They didn't expect us, but we managed to find some beds belonging to blokes on leave. No doubt profanity filled the air when our cheeky apologies for the use of their comforts were conveyed to them.

No peace for the wicked. 6 a.m. next morning saw us awake and numbers in the air within a quarter of an hour, still rubbing tired eyes and yawning too. The "kytes" had been worked on all through the night by a small bloody keen bunch of grease monkeys. And all the technical hitches had been unknotted.

This time it was an entirely different aerodrome, at "M," that we used for a forward base, but the scenery when we'd landed was entirely the same as the view from the tarmac at "G." Aeroplanes to the right of me, aeroplanes to the left of me, aeroplanes in front, in fact, acroplanes. It was quite comforting to see this local display of might, and we all had a feeling of confident optimism that, whatever happened, the sparks would certainly fly, given half a chance. I (and the others) had been here before and knew the general layout, but it didn't matter since we didn't get the chance to stray any distance from our machines.

A cup of tea was available, at this unearthly hour, from a N.A.A.F.I. van. The time of day, coupled with the fact that the beverage was gratis, caused us much speculation as to the coming trip.

The various C.O.'s of the participating squadrons had visited the Ops. Room, where the general scheme was outlined to them and they, in their turn, made arrangements for mutual safety and efficiency. Once more, so we were told, we were to be "stooge" squadron of the group, which would be stepped-up, squadron at a time, at intervals of about 4,000 feet. We estimated that taking-off as quickly as was safe we would all be in the correct position when we crossed the coast S.E. There was no need for the squadron-leader to say, "Have you all got that?" since we'd now had two days' practice at being "good Samaritans," besides which it's remarkable the interest in the finer points one takes when life might be suddenly terminated.

The morning was fresh with haze up to about 4,000 feet and between that and 6,000 feet there were some patchy bits of cloud. In fact, a typical summer's morning, that foretold a brilliant day of sunshine, which indeed it turned out to be. Getting away was done surprisingly quick considering our machines were mixed amongst the mob generally. A little "pedalling" on the rudder-bar, plenty of hard pressure on the brake-lever and we had taxied clear of the other parked aircraft, amidst a cloud of dust, since this particular station was noted for its dry soil qualities.

We took off in "vic's" of three aircraft. Jock was No. 2 on the right, with myself on the left as No.3 of our section, which was led by a daring but experienced flying-officer. We were termed "Yellow" section, and brought up the rear of the four sections which comprised the squadron. The others being Blue, leading, followed by Green and Red sections.

Very quickly we took up our positions, and when Blue Leader, the C.O., called up over the "R/T," "Are you in position Green, Red and Yellow leaders?" all were able to reply in the affirmative. As we climbed up, circling the aerodrome, we were given a precautionary warning to use the weak mixture to conserve our fuel, and also be sparing with oxygen. Meanwhile the other squadrons were following in our wake, having taken-off behind us.

The intention was to cross the English coast at 7 a.m., all stationed correctly at our prearranged heights – 27,000 feet for us. By this time the squadron-leader had earned the title of "Oxygen Charlie," owing to our close proximity to the celestial bodies on each of these shows. The actual sweep over French soil was to last an hour, since our fuel supply wouldn't leave us a good fighting margin if this period were exceeded.

Whilst we were gaining height, every one settled down, and I found myself doing the routine things such as trimming the aircraft to fly nicely to the hand, adjusting the seat and straps for safety and comfort, setting the gun-sights, and switching on the necessary heaters which neutralise the cold at high altitude, so preventing freezing-up of the instruments. I found myself very apprehensive. Would we meet anything this time? I wondered if the Jerries are as crafty as they say in using the sun and extra height. Anyhow I'd much rather be up here than one of those poor blighters on the beach at Dunkirk. I visualised the morning papers of the past few days, each prominently displaying a map of the battle area, the same area to which we were heading, and each showing a complete encirclement of the Dunkirk locality by German armoured divisions. Why had we been trapped like it – were the German chiefs too clever, or was it muddling; if the latter, WHY?

In much the same way as in a dream my mind seemed to flit from thought to thought, sometimes with no fixed relationship, and constantly running through the advice of more experienced pilots: If they get on your tail – go into a steep turn and make it steep – try to climb and gain height – you'll beat 'em. And so it went on.

After about 20 minutes the dial registering the oxygen content in its cylinder showed an abnormally large drop, compared with what I had usually experienced. The supply gauge, on the other hand, showed itself to be perfectly normal, so I immediately knew that there must be a leak somewhere in the pipe-line or system, and it was odds on that the oxygen would run out on me. However, not wanting to be out of it, I elected to carry on until it really did get empty, and proceeded to use a supply equivalent to a height of 5,000 feet below that at which we were flying, in an attempt to economise. It gave me a slight headache for a short while, but an occasional burst of the correct amount seemed to overcome that.

We crossed the coast outward bound only a minute or so behind schedule and were now flying in fairly open formation with us "Yellow" boys behind, and a bit above the rest of the squadron. Thus Yellow section could act as lookouts for the squadron against attacks from above.

I saw nothing of the other squadrons or any other aircraft as we swept over the Channel and carried out our patrol, and I was watching the oxygen very carefully. After about fifty minutes of the patrol it was down on the red danger mark, indicating that it was almost empty. Without oxygen at 27,000 feet I would pass out in very short time, so I was about to call up my C.O. for permission to return home, when another high-pitched, excited voice smote my ears before I could speak: "Hallo, Blue Leader, Red Leader calling, I can see something going on below, am going down to investigate" – a short pause then a reply – "O.K. Red

Leader, Yellow section follow and guard their tails." That meant us, and it was the answer to my oxygen troubles since I could manage without any if I went low enough.

"Here it is," I thought. "Hell! Yellow one's putting on the horses." By this time, however, we had lost sight of Reds as they had a slight lead, and their camouflage soon merged into the terrain below. However, we dived like "ding-bats," making it almost impossible to keep formation decently. Jock and I were quite wide from our leader as we tore through some patchy cloud at 15,000 feet using both hands on the stick. This cloud proved a bloody nuisance, as our ice-cold windscreens misted up with frozen water vapour on the inside, and I could see 3/5 of "Fanny Adams."

At about 12,000 feet we saw several batches of bombers – HE. 111 and JU. 88's – sweeping around the area in threes and fives. Yellow 1 yelled out, "Prepare for No. 3 attack," one which we had practised so often and hadn't been put to the test. Next, "Line astern – GO!" came over the radio, as we weaved round into position to attack 5 JU. 88's who appeared oblivious of our presence. Next came the precautionary order, "Echelon port – GO!" just as I noticed a lot of ack-ack popping up 330 yards behind the enemy. The French were going great guns but not hitting anything. Perhaps they thought we were enemy fighters – perhaps. Why is it, I ruminated, that the anti-aircraft gun is designed to shoot where the bombers *have* been and not where they are. Surely a good intelligent chap could give them just an extra bit of elevation and range, merely by looking at the results. But then I'm only a lay mind and it's no doubt much more difficult really.

Anyway, ignoring the "muck," we forged our way up

astern of the 88's and pumped lead into them on a grand scale. In order to see my target I had to continually rub my windscreens with my gauntlet as the forward view was completely obscured by water which had frozen. I rubbed clear a small patch sufficient to see through, but I had to keep rubbing as the frost formed up as quickly as I removed it. It's a sod holding the "stick" in one hand and rubbing away with the other. If I don't look out I'll misjudge my distance and ram that ugly load of hate in front. And yet I don't seem to be overtaking him very fast. Quite nice in fact, a tribute to the leading of Yellow 1. It's grand to sit there and hear a noise like taut canvas ripping as the eight guns send out flashing white streaks towards their objective. The machine I myself selected and attacked, as far as I could see, had jets of flame and black smoke trailing back from its engines, and was certainly badly damaged. Our leader broke off the attack sideways and downwards in the approved fashion, with No. 2 and myself following in close attendance, then climbed up again to position himself for a further attack. I wondered what was being said and done in the bomber meanwhile.

It was whilst I was trailing Nos. 1 and 2 in this climb that I spotted a silver Messerschmitt 109 single-engine fighter circling into position to have a crack at me from the rear. Giving the others a yell over the "R/T," accompanied by a display of blue lights from my posterior (which would have been the envy of Mr. Brock), I wheeled away into a super-tight left-hand turn which appeared too much for him since he sheered off at plus boost; I presume to try and surprise another stooge.

I had only just rid myself of this pest when huge white

plumes of smoke began streaming back past the hood from the direction of the engine exhaust. I immediately concluded that the French had hit something at last, or possibly a JU. 88 had scored a "double top" on my engine with their return fire. A quick glance at the instruments assured me that the engine was as rough as it felt, with the radiator temp. well around the "clock" on its second trip, together with a negligible oil pressure. When black smoke and oil fumes suddenly enveloped me from the direction of my feet blotting out everything and almost suffocating me, I realised that I shouldn't see my base, or even the white cliffs of England, that day again.

After a struggle I slipped the hood back against the vacuum effect of the slip stream. This action served to drive all the smoke and filth back to the bottom of the cockpit, and cleared my head a bit. I switched off the engine to decrease the risk of fire and a petrol-tank explosion, then, assuming a nice gliding speed and performing a series of turns, I surveyed the earth below for a suitable landing-ground. The beach first sprang to mind, but this was out definitely as every few yards was littered with wrecked aircraft and boats. The sea I didn't relish as I thought the chances of rescue would be remote and since there seemed practically no sea-borne craft in the vicinity. French fields looked uncommonly small and dangerous from 6-7,000 feet, so the only alternative was baling out.

Not wishing to be on the end of a "brolly" for any length of time in case I became a nice juicy bit of 109 meat, I chose to glide to a safe minimum height before "walking out." It was funny not to see myself "panic" as I always imagined would happen in a crisis. I now look back and think, "Well, who would have thought it." I suppose the fact that such possibilities as the state I was now in had been discussed so much, and that with certain routines in emergency it took away a hell of a lot of the cause for fear. I had just removed my helmet and released my safety harness when, as luck would have it, I caught sight of something which looked far more like another silver 109 than a liver spot. He regarded me as easy prey, no doubt, and began to approach my tail from above to port. Without engine there was only one thing I could do. A sharp diving turn brought me straight into the huge pall of black smoke which stretched up to nearly 5,000 feet from the blazing oil tanks in the Dunkirk docks area. When I emerged into sunshine again on the other side of the smoke, my friend the 109 had disappeared. He probably thought I was a "goner" and left it at that, thank God!

When I was about 2,000 feet, and with the airspeed at 180 m.p.h., I started to abandon aircraft in the manner so often discussed and recommended in the pilots' room. The idea was to turn the aircraft on to its back, then drop out, pulling the "ring" at one's own convenience. The thing which hadn't been stressed, but which proved the most important, was that the "harness" should remain fastened until the last moment, when, on extracting the release-pin, gravity (according to the venerable Mr. Newton) should assist exit.

As I've already explained, the harness which should have been tight was already off. As a result, in attempting to invert the machine, yours truly found himself three-quarters of the way over and unable to go either way. A very chaotic state of mind prevailed. However, a fortunate lapse of memory excludes the hectic happening of the next few seconds. A vague remembrance of having two attempts to push myself out, and the next I knew was that I wouldn't have to take the chute back as a "dud" after all. Mentally the parachute packer was awarded about 15 V.C.s and a brace of life-saving certificates.

The fun wasn't over yet though. Oh no! There were still French military below and they gave me the benefit of a sneaking burst of machine-gun fire. Fortunately, like their "heavy stuff," this was just as accurate. It didn't hit the "brolly" even. I learned later that a solo occupant leaving a British fighter was regarded as a parachutist (German version). This impression apparently still existed when I hit terra firma between two tin huts in a village factory at Fermini. For no sooner had I released my chute when I was set upon by a group of chattering niggers, Moroccan employees, I believe. About four grabbed me and another three saw to it that my gun didn't leave its holster. I was vainly protesting my innocence and nationality when, lo and behold! one of these dark-skinned individuals was creeping up behind the party feeling furtively in the folds of his overalls. It wasn't a bad life while it lasted, I reflected, and was about to make a last despairing effort when up dashed a "poilu" whom I afterwards regarded as the spirit of common sense. He took command, and with the retinue of "wog" workers I was escorted back to his unit's head-quarters – a commandeered house. Here I established my identity with a mixture of broken French and gesticulations, also earning the complete confidence and approval of our dusky thugs. I learned that their religion demands decapitation as the only indication of death. We do see life.

At the H.Q. officers' dug-out, amidst all the

pandemonium of dive-bombing and shelling, a couple of Jersey boys proved good pals as well as interpreters. They asked for news of the war and the day of the week, since the hurried retreat had meant the loss of all sense of time and place. I supplied what information I could without disclosing that I thought they hadn't much chance of getting out of the offensive circle put up by the Germans.

They in turn told me that they were moving into Dunkirk that afternoon and would take me with them. I was anxious to get cracking but had to wait meanwhile, getting my first meal of the day in the form of horse-flesh and unsettled French wine.

Well, in due course one of the Jersey chaps took me to the French H.Q. in Dunkirk in an Austin 8 which they had retrieved from the ditch.

Chaos ruled everywhere. Hundreds of vehicles of war graced both sides of the road, where they had been abandoned as a hindrance by previous owners and drivers. Cattle and a few horses stampeded about the field, littered with decaying bodies of their contemporaries who had been hit by shrapnel or blast. Here and there one saw a car ditched, riddled with bullet holes, and now and again a body of a refugee who had been "caught-up with." A sordid journey from start to finish, and considering my movements the previous 24 hours it all seemed a dream.

After further questioning at the French G.H.Q. I was conveyed to the British G.H.Q. at a site nearer the docks. Here were heavy guns of the dock's defence belching forth, more often than not, premature explosions. Ruin and desolation faced me at every turn, but negotiating wrecked buildings I was eventually deposited amongst a most comforting sight, the first British people I had seen that day. At the G.H.Q., to my surprise, I met none other than Jock who had also been shot down and wounded slightly too. That I should meet a fellow pilot was no end of a tonic. We alternately sat and lay flat in a semi-underground shelter for the next few hours, until we were told to make our way to the mole under our own steam. This was a painfully slow business for Jock, and we had to shelter two or three times under vehicles whilst the mole was subjected to continuous shelling and dive-bombing. On one side of the road were blazing railway trucks, goods yards, and shipyards, whilst away on the right was the huge cloud of black smoke rising from the oil tanks in the distance on the other side of the mole.

Once after sheltering in a "casualty station," we looked out to find a lorry which had sheltered us two minutes before now a mass of twisted wreckage spread over an area five times its normal size. All in the day's work to the Army boys, but a sensational "birthday" for us.

Eventually the docks were reached and we were greeted by a very cheery bunch of Tars, who seemed to have established permanent residence amongst a pile of sandbags. Another revolting sight was unfolded when some French soldiers began shooting all the stray dogs, insisting they were message-carriers. They did it in the painful way, with about four shots, afterwards dropping the tormented things into the water. I suspected that more than one of the Tommies would willingly have set to on the French had it not been for the futility of it all in the circumstances.

At about 8.30, after about 12 hours or more on French soil, Admiral W——W—— instructed Jock and myself to jump aboard a launch which had moored alongside some

50 yards farther down the quay. Not being master mariners and with Jock wounded, the game of descending 30 feet or so to water-level proved quite a problem, but once aboard, the Senior Service made us extremely comfortable. We went to sleep in luxurious bunks (for a weapon of war). An hour later we were awakened and transferred to a destroyer which with two more of its kind had come alongside to take off what was the rear party of the British evacuation. Even the G.H.Q. was finishing, and after that night Dunkirk would be totally French. So 12 hours later would have even more seriously curtailed our chances of rescue had we baled-out the next day.

The five-hour journey to Dover wasn't entirely without incident. Twice the ship's guns blazed at an aircraft, probably laying mines in our path, besides which some curious chap on the deck above had tried the trigger of his rifle, with rather disastrous results for a second-lieutenant who sat in the chair of the mess-room below, which the officers and wounded were sharing. I myself had given up the chair only a bare fifteen minutes earlier. Another of those miracles of fate which in these troubled times seem an everyday occurrence.

2 a.m. saw us back on English soil and given every help by a bunch of hard-working civilians and service folk.

Some sandwiches, tea and then to the Lord W. Hotel, where we communicated the news of our return from the dead to a very sleepy controller at our parent base. After that in brilliant moonlight we made our way to a rest centre for a few hours' sleep after a day crammed full of excitement and suspense. Truly a "Channel packet."

INTRODUCING DUREX

Durex is really a most extraordinary character. On the whole his appearance is pretty tidy – shortish, and slicks his hair, but he has got one of those comic faces that looks as if it was made of rubber, with a large mouth and broken nose – not what one would call handsome according to Grecian standards, or any other standards for that matter. He is the clown of the squadron, a man who imitates every noise, from an underground train pulling in and out of a station to the recochetting of a rifle bullet (American movie style). No matter where we were, no matter what was happening, there was a constant barrage of back-chat coming from Durex with intermittent ricochetting bullets. Even at dawn readiness you never got rid of this constant burble. You would see him walking down the tarmac all by himself, his mouth working feverishly, and as he approached you would hear all sorts of extraordinary sounds. He could take-off a cockney to perfection and simply delighted in "poking Charlie" at any stray workmen on the aerodrome. I was always surprised that the workmen didn't resent some of the things he said to them, but they took it in fun.

As a pilot one could hardly class him as being exceptional, but he had plenty of guts, and was always flat-out to have a crack at something, the only trouble about this being, of course, that he very seldom shot anything down himself – he invariably got shot up. I don't remember a single occasion on which we made contact with the enemy and Durex got home without at least one bullet hole in his machine.

He was a good party type and could keep people amused on the ride home better than anybody I have ever come across, but there is no doubt about it, a little of Durex went a long way.

"O.K. I've got her," and round we would go again. These are the words that I remember the most in my whole flying career.

When I first learned to fly and tried landing a "kite," I never seemed to be able to keep the thing on the ground. Round and round the aerodrome I would go and still I hadn't gone solo. I would go home at night, feeling thoroughly fed-up with life. It was in peace-time, and I was learning to fly with the V.R.s.

My folks at home gave me great encouragement, and one morning just before lunch I made it——

Now began my flying career. I was a pilot flying on my own and was determined to make a good show of it – but did I ever, for a moment, imagine that I should be a fighter-pilot! I hoped I would, but didn't picture anything so great as a Spitfire.

Then came the War! and sixteen weeks of no flying at all. I was sent to C——, where I wore out a considerable amount of shoe (boot) leather on the roads there, marching about like a bloody soldier and not as a sergeant-pilot; but in the evenings we made up for it with some very "wet" parties.

Well, to cut a long story short, there followed my E.F.T.S. course, where I finished off my Tiger Moth flying, my I.T.S. and F.T.S. courses, where I passed out with my Wings and a good flying report, and also a commission –

goodness only knows why, but still there it was. On to my dream at O.T.U., where I learned to fly a Spitfire.

August 31st, 1940. After a very hectic week-end in London, I returned in a semi-fogged condition to the O.T.U. Station, and was informed I was to report to a squadron.

Nothing very much happened during the month which followed. I learned how to use my guns properly and fly in good formation.

September 29th, 1940. My birthday. I was informed at dispersal hut that I was to pack my things and after lunch leave to join "Clickerty- Click" Squadron. Little did I know that I should be leaving a place that I thought quite good fun, to join a bunch of lads that had got the right ideas about fighting, and enjoying the lighter side of life at the same time.

September 30th, 1940. I arrived at "G" aerodrome at about 10 o'clock in the morning and met everybody. I was rather impressed, because they were the only squadron to be stationed there.

The C.O. at once asked me what I was going to have to drink.

It was at this point that I got my nickname of "Durex" – a tough bull-necked fellow called "Bogle" christened me. Afterwards, we became great friends. He was an excellent pilot, and would come back to the aerodrome on many occasions with his machine riddled with bullets and nearly falling to pieces.

By this time I was fully operational, and very keen to get up and have a crack at these ME. 109's with which they had been having fun. I should, first, mention the fellows who were in the squadron at the time – these will be all nicknames, of course. In the same flight as myself, namely "A," there was Bogle, Butch, as well as several others, Apple and the flight-commander, Ken.

I talked quite a lot with these chaps about their methods of attack, and learned all about the more practical methods that were being used by the squadron.

October 1st. Was allowed to go up and "have a crack," but to my dismay we did not see a thing. The weather was perfect, and we flew at about 30,000 feet most of the time.

October 2nd. As far as I can remember we took off in the morning at about 11 o'clock and climbed north to gain height. They informed us from the ground that there were quite a lot of Huns about. As we went up, I clearly remember setting my sights and turning my gun-button to "Fire."

We had gained height and were flying south towards the coast when I saw above us some pairs of what I thought were ME. 109's. I was flying "tail-end Charlie" at the time, and was surprised to see the squadron go into line astern as if going to the attack, and turn to starboard and downwards. I then did a very silly thing, as I learned afterwards. I left the squadron and climbed towards the nearest 109.

As I did so, I kept a keen look-out on all sides for any others that might take a pot at me. They were painted a brown colour on top and all white underneath – I noticed this as I closed in on them. As I reached about 32,000 feet, I got into range on one chap who was flying across my nose and above me. My sights were not working, but I allowed as far as I could for deflection and opened fire. My shots were a bit wide at first, but using my tracer carefully, I could bring the shots to bear on him. After two or three bursts, he suddenly half-rolled to the left and dived. I was, of course, below him, so I throttled back and did the same. As I did so, I was amazed to see that instead of continuing to dive he levelled out, presenting himself as an excellent target: I could see my incendiary bullets hitting all round the cockpit. It gave me a great thrill at the time. Then, suddenly, things began to happen to the Jerry. I couldn't make them out at first, but when the hood flew open and I saw the pilot leave the plane with a stream of white trailing behind, I knew that I had got my first Hun – was I thrilled, or was I? I can remember shouting at the top of my voice and feeling very pleased with myself. Then, and not until then, I began to think of looking around for the rest of the chaps, and also to see if there were any other Huns about. The sky was clear, so I dived down to where I hoped I should find the wreckage of my Hun. I came through the cloud at about 2,000 feet and saw a column of smoke rising from a hillside, so I went over and investigated.

Yes, it was the wreckage of some machine or other: I hoped it was mine. Anyway, I then flew home very content and full of what I was going to tell my young brother and the folks at home.

When I got back to the mess, Bogle, who had been on leave and therefore wasn't flying, asked me how I had got on. I wasn't quite sure how to begin actually. I didn't want to "shoot a hell of a line" on my first week (although that should worry me: I'm about the biggest line-shooter in the squadron now). So I said to him, "Have any of the others come back yet?" "No," he said. "Did you see anything?" I replied, "Yes, as a matter of fact, we saw about 8 or 9 109's." Full of enthusiasm, he said, "Did you have a crack at 'em?" I replied again, "Yes, I did." "Any luck?" "Well, the pilot baled-out, so I suppose it was O.K." He laughed and slapped me on the back, and there followed drinks all round. Bogle at that period had got about five to his credit, so I looked upon him as a bit of an ace.

When the C.O. and the rest returned, he was surprised when they all told him I had got one, because they hadn't seen any at all.

For the rest of that day we did some more patrols, but did not have any further engagements.

October 4th, 1940. It was a cloudy day and we did not carry out any large formation patrols.

By this time, I had got pretty well settled down with the boys. We used to sleep out of camp in the next village, and travelled backwards and forwards by lorry. Being the only squadron there, we were on readiness nearly every morning, which meant getting up at about 5.30 and sleeping in the mess until breakfast-time.

It was whilst we were there that quite a few cups and glasses were broken by Bogle and myself. We used to wait until one of us was unprepared and then chuck a plate across the room, at the same time shouting "Catch" at the top of our voices. The other would spin round usually too late, and to the amusement of the assembled company, the cup or what-have-you would crash to the ground. Very childish – but it gave us a good laugh. That is an interesting point, really. I noticed that with all the periods of waiting about, and long hours sometimes with nothing to do, nerves got a bit strained, and for sheer mental and physical relief one had to shout or break something – and, believe you me, it was a grand relief too. Another form of amusement was to go to the pictures in a large body and at appropriate points in the show shout something out, usually verging on the low.

We had in the mess at that time a large radiogram with quite a few records, most of them belonging to Bogle. This used to be playing nearly all day; the C.O.'s favourite was Dorothy Lamour singing "These Foolish Things." Most chaps had their favourite tunes with hot "dames" or "broads" singing them.

The "tannoy" there was controlled from the mess, so we used to stick the mike in front of the speaker and I'm sure they could hear it down in the town.

Another amusing occupation that we performed at periods of rest and when we felt "brassed off" was the games of poker that we used to get up.

We used to stake money on anything; horses and cards were our favourites with the occasional Dog Derbys as well.

After lunch on this particular day, there was a call for two aircraft to "scramble" Maidstone 15,000 feet. So Bogle and I dashed to our machines. "F" was mine at the time. The cloud went up in layers to 15,000 feet, where it was perfectly clear. We proceeded for the next hour or so to fly from 2,000 to anything up to 15,000, and after this hour, feeling very fed up, were ordered to return to base.

Fortunately, after I had landed, I didn't switch off my wireless, and heard the controller tell Bogle to stay up there as there was one Jerry still about. I thought, "Blast this for a game of darts," and took off again. Not finding my leader, I thought the only place the Hun would be would most probably be above cloud, so I started to climb.

As I emerged from cloud over London, I sighted a two-engined craft "stooging" over the town. I felt sure this was a Hun; my heart missed about three beats as I pointed the nose of my Spit. in its direction. Setting my sights for JU. 88, I felt sure it would be one. According to the powers that be, the blokes what know or the aces, I then did a very foolish thing – instead of hopping in and out of cloud and stalking the swine, I flew straight up to him and at about 400 to 300 yards opened fire with a slight deflection shot.

The "E/A" immediately dived for cloud (he *was* an 88 by the way) with myself hard on his tail. I got really annoyed with him, because he was going very fast, and I didn't seem to be doing any damage, although I was pumping lead into him as hard as I could go. I spotted tracer leaving my port outer gun (that is what I thought). On looking more closely, it wasn't my bullets at all, but a spot of return fire from the rear gunner. Boy! was I shaken! I then proceeded to "rub the guy out," as they say, but before I could get cracking, he had reached cloud. What was I to do? Follow, or what? I thought that he might come above cloud again, so I flattened out; by this time I had reached another layer of head-cloud, or I should say a corridor between two layers. There below and just behind on the left I spotted my Hun still diving. I wiped the kite over into a steep left-hand turn and endeavoured to get on his tail again.

At this point I flashed past a Spitfire, but was too intent on the bloke in front to wonder whether it was my leader or not. As it happened it was, and afterwards Bogie said that I shot past like a thing possessed. He got away in cloud again, and this time I didn't see him again. I continued diving and set out for the coast in the hope of sighting him again on the way home – but no luck! I just had to be content with shooting-a-line. This gentle art had become quite a favourite of mine by this time; in fact, I had become quite an ace – to my own mind, that is.

October 5th, 1940. About this time (I can't quite remember the exact dates but as far as I can remember) Bob and Bogle got their D.F.C.'s, much to the great enthusiasm of all the rest of us. Bogle had to his credit about 13 unconfirmed 109's, many of which he last saw spinning for cloud on fire. These he could not confirm. We used to pull his leg no end about the "lines" that used to appear in the papers about his decoration!

On the 4th October, my flight-commander went out with two others, the names of which I forget off-hand, after a Heinkel III and he failed to return. His body was washed-up about a week or so later; a very fine chap he was too, and one of the best shots in the R.A.F. also. If he had lived, he would most probably be a D.S.O., D.F.C. "type," by now.

After this, "Cookie" took over the flight. He had once been shot down in flames – the scars could still be seen on his face then. He was a good pilot and a good leader; also, he was very fond of odd games of poker.

On this particular day, I think I was flying as his No. 3 or it may have been that I was "tail-end Charlie!" I was usually put there, because I joined the squadron as a fully operational pilot.

Well, we had been stooging around for an hour or more, when we sighted a formation of 109's, about fifteen of 'em, below us, thank goodness. Most of them were usually above by the time we arrived on the scene.

Things happened fast; the boys went into line astern, and I, being above the squadron, dropped down into the best open space in the formation.

I vividly remember seeing on this particular trip an ME. streaking for the ground with black smoke pouring from its yellow-nosed engine, hotly pursued by a Spitfire. Boy! what a thrilling sight. I think I shouted, "Atta boy, give him hell, chum," or words to that effect. Machines split up and went in all directions – the fight was on. I followed one of the boys down until I spotted a 109 going for home. I immediately got on to his tail and was after him like a dog for its dinner.

Closing to about 300 or 400 yards, I opened fire, the bullets roared out over the noise of the engine. They don't rattle like an ordinary Army Vickers gun. No sir! When the 8 Brownings open fire – what a thrill! The smoke whips back into the cockpit and sends a thrill running down your spine.

The Jerry seemed to jump in the air and start a gradual descent. I followed, giving short bursts. As I closed upon him, I saw that we were overtaking another 109 at a slightly greater height than we were.

I didn't fancy being shot up the back by this one, so I left my Jerry to his fate, and opened fire upon the second. Nothing much happened to him and by this time we were overtaking a third, this one being also higher and to the right. I held my fire after breaking away from No. 2 and put a burst into No. 3. He semi-half rolled and dived for the coast. Opening my throttle, I was after him, also giving short burst. This one then suddenly climbed for the sun. As he did so, I pulled my nose up and had him cold. I pressed the button . . . nothing happened. I had run out of ammunition. Did I swear? I'll say.

To my surprise, the Jerry flattened out and began to glide down again. I presumed he was gliding because I began to overtake him. . . . Throttling back so that I could see what would happen to him . . . hoping against hope that I should see him crash into the sea.

At this point everything seemed quiet, but I'm afraid "all was not gold that glittered" at that moment. There was, all of a sudden, a terrific explosion inside the cockpit, and smoke seemed to be coming from the engine – not the smell of my guns, but an acrid stench. "What the hell was that?" I thought, and checked my instruments. At that moment I knew all right what it was when a shower of bullets hit my aircraft and something banged my leg with a sickening thud. I didn't wait to see "who threw that," but did a complete half-roll to the left and went down in a tight spiral turn, craning my neck to see if there was anything on my tail.

When I reached about 10,000 feet (this all happened at about 25,000 feet) I flattened out, and boy! was I sweating. I collected my thoughts together and prepared to check my aircraft for damage – checking flaps and nothing happened; then trying my wheels, I found they only came down half-way. I put them up and set course for base. My hydraulic system had been hit and my right trouser leg and flying boot were covered in oil – anti-freeze, Mark II, or whatever it is.

By this time my left leg was beginning to ache a bit, so I decided to see what damage was done there. I couldn't see anything and my boot seemed to be O.K. Feeling inside, I felt blood soaking through my sock – right, now I knew that I had been hit – how badly I couldn't tell. Winding the rudder bias so that my right leg took all the weight, I prepared for my landing.

Approaching the 'drome, I set all my gadgets and put the undercart lever in the "down" position; it only went down half-way, so I decided to use the emergency CO_2 bottle. This brought it right down and locked it.

I then made my circuit and at the appropriate time turned in to land; my landing speed was very fast, because of course I had no flaps. As I neared the ground, I realised that it would be rather a hazard landing, as my windscreen was covered with this oil, rendering my forward vision very bad.

As she sank, I realised I was holding off too high, so I had to give it a short burst of engine to lower it gently to the ground. By this time I was half-way across the very small 'drome and looked like running off the edge.

Fortunately for me, my right tyre was punctured, so as I ran along I was pulled to the right, which slowed me up considerably. When I climbed out the ambulance came tearing up and I was taken to the M.O. Actually, it was a surface wound – the bullet had come from the back of the aircraft and passed through my boot, cutting a nice furrow in the fleshy part of my leg, and continuing out of the front of my boot.

The C.O. decided that I had better have a day off, so I packed up my things and set off for home, feeling rather an ass on the quiet.

October 7th, 1940. It was about this time that we were flying pretty long hours. On this particular morning, I can remember we were up at about 4.45, and most of us slept or dozed in the arm-chairs in the mess.

At about 06.00, we were ordered off, the whole squadron, and we were up for about an hour. We didn't see anything though, and we were very glad to get down and have some breakfast.

Well, as it happened, we didn't get very far with this bunfight before we were ordered off again. I had just finished my porridge when the order came through. It is rather fun to see a scramble, as it is called. Plates and knives go down with a bang; every one reaches the door at the same moment, and you filter through as best you can. "Mae West's" are grabbed and one tears towards one's aircraft shouting, "Start up 'J'," or whatever machine you're flying. This patrol was also uneventful – we did not see any Huns.

Well, at about 10.00 hours, I sat down to my bacon and eggs, thinking to myself, "Well, that's that for a bit. I guess I can enjoy my spot of eats," but, oh no! After I had finished my second course the phone rang and up we had to go again. I tried to force some hot tea down, but the C.O. wouldn't let me, so you can see how quickly we used to get out to our aeroplanes. Actually from the time we left the table to the time all the 12 aircraft left the ground wasn't more than three to four minutes.

On this trip we were stooging around for about an hour and a half, but although there were plenty of Jerry's about, we didn't see any.

Down we came again, and this time got a lounge in the chairs in the mess. At about 11 o'clock cocoa was brought round and we all had a tuck-in. At about 11.30 we were ordered off again.

This time up we went to 30 thou' and stooged about a

bit up there. After we had been up for about 30 minutes, I spotted lots of pairs of what looked like ME. 109's flying harmlessly above us.

After a time the squadron seemed to be going down. I tried to call them up and tell them about these chaps above us, but no – I think my R/T must have failed, and up I went on my own. I had been flying above the squadron, as usual.

As I climbed up after a pair that were going north, I suddenly spotted a yellow nose on my immediate starboard, so that I was to him a full deflection target. I thought to myself, "Oh, I don't think he'll get me," so I pulled into a steeper climbing turn just in case – but it was too late!

The next thing that happened was the horrid thump as the bullets and cannon shells hit my aircraft. At the same moment, I felt a terrific bang on my side and right arm, coupled with that acrid stench of cordite which always seems to follow when one is hit. I half rolled to the right and dived for the ground, going down in ever-decreasing circles. I then straightened out and took stock of my surroundings and damage. I checked my wheels and flap – this time I had no wheel pressure, but the flaps were O.K. My engine temperatures were also all right. Oil temp. about 75 to 80, pressure 90 lbs., but looking out to my starboard I could see that a cannon shell had caught my aileron very nicely and it was in shreds, with lumps of canvas streaming off it.

I tested my control – everything seemed O.K. The *last* time my machine had been holed with bullets from stern to stem. There were shots into the metal prop. too, and several control wires had been cut. This time my control column was well over to the right and the machine was flying straight and level. I tested the lateral control fairly accurately because I thought, "I'll save as much of this machine as I can, because I can land it on its belly, and the engine will be O.K. anyway."

My side began to hurt like hell at that time. I thought that I was really hurt this time and began to think to myself, "This bloody war isn't quite so funny as I thought it was." I spotted an aerodrome which is just out of Maidstone, and made for that. Why I didn't get home I don't know, but my only thought at that time was to "plonk" it down at the nearest aerodrome I could find.

So, preparing for a landing 20,000 feet below, I started to glide down. As I reached about 2,000 feet I began to get worried about my aileron. It wasn't till I had got all that way and realised that if anything had happened near the ground it would have been the end – or, as we say, "I should have had it."

Everything went off to plan. I didn't bother to circle the aerodrome, but tried my wheels – nothing happened, so I then put my flaps down and tightened my straps ready for the shock as the machine hit the ground.

As I went over the hedge, I caught a glimpse of upturned faces – they were watching me coming in without wheels. I did a normal landing and braced myself for the bump; the machine slid about twenty yards and then came to a standstill – there was rather an unpleasant smell as the engine, now fairly hot, burned the oil around the cylinder block. I sat there for a moment, and then, switching everything off and checking all my switches, climbed out.

My side began to ache like hell about this time, and my arm ached so that I couldn't hold anything with it.

As the ambulance came on the scene I checked that my parachute and helmet were being looked after properly, but the M.O. hurried me into the ambulance and said, "That's O.K., don't worry – we'll send them on to your unit," which, incidentally, they did, much to my gratitude, as I found out when I returned to base.

I was taken down to the sick quarters, where they tended my wounds. As I went there in the ambulance, I tried to think how badly I had been hurt. When I got there they took my shirt off and all that had happened was that I had got about four pieces of cannon shell in my side. Very small and doing very little damage. Why I felt so bad was because they had penetrated the muscles and bruised me and made my side ache more than if I had actually been hit really well.

Well, I felt a bit of an idiot, and was carted off to a very nice country house that had been turned into a hospital.

I was in hospital for about a week and had quite a pleasant but well-needed rest. When I got back, the C.O. said he was very pleased to see me back again and that I should have a few days off, and as we were stationed near my home, I could have four days, if I wished. I took 'em, and had quite a nice time. Mind you, I was able to "shoot a pretty good line," it being the second time I was shot down.

October 16th, 1940. Returned to the squadron after my leave and discovered the facts that I have just narrated. For the days following we didn't have any luck at all. At this time I was very eager to have another scrap and see how I felt. Having been shot down twice fairly close on one another, I began to wonder how the next packet would arrive.

October 17th, 1940. New C.O. took over.

October 25th, 1940. My tense feeling was very much relieved when on this day we sighted two formations of 109's.

It was a cloudy day, low down, but above 5,000 feet it was as clear as a bell. We climbed up to 30,000 feet and sighted a small formation of ME.s about 2,000 feet below us and coming in from the coast. We went into line astern and attacked. I followed my leader down and then thought I saw an ME. ahead of me, but on reaching 15,000 feet I realised it was only a Spitfire.

I was very annoyed at losing all that well-needed height without seeing anything and immediately looked around for some of the boys. I could only find one, so I joined up with him and signalled him to commence to climb when I spotted some smoke trails above us; these I thought or hoped were our boys and climbed towards them, taking care to approach from the rear in case they were hostile.

At about 28,000 feet I could recognise them as Spitfires, and continued to join up with them. Meanwhile the other chap, a sergeant, "bogged off" some place – I didn't see him again that trip.

As I joined up, I couldn't see any vacant places, so I called up the C.O. and said I would like to take up position as "weaver."

We were then turning north, and I reckoned that it wouldn't be long before they would tell us to land again, and was beginning to get rather disheartened when they told us there were some "Snappers" in our immediate vicinity.

Suddenly we saw them; they were steering in groups of four, line-astern, their yellow noses shining in the sun.

Every one seemed to split up and attack something. I found myself above and looked around well, left and right, and in my mirror to make sure nobody was on my tail.

Then I spotted four 109's approaching me from the starboard quarter. I thought to myself, "I don't want that lot shooting at me with cannons, etc.," so I pulled away to one side and climbed a bit. I let them file past and then turned on the tail of the last bloke. (I missed a very good chance of getting more than one on that trip. I should have turned sooner than I did and held a long burst so that all four should pass through it.) Anyway, I put in a short sharp full deflection shot on the last Jerry but didn't have time to see any results. He dived off from the others, going almost straight down and not rolling over to the left or right. I followed, and gave short bursts as I went. The speed was gradually increasing so I hadn't much chance of drawing any closer. I fired burst after burst, but still nothing happened. At last he pushed his nose down even farther and started to wobble a bit, finally disappearing into cloud with a stream of white smoke pouring from the starboard side of the engine.

I knew that the cloud was about 5,000 feet so decided that I wouldn't follow in a steep dive, so commenced to turn in a spiral. I came out of cloud at about 2,000 feet and searched for the E/A but couldn't find him. After giving my report on return I got this as a probable.

October 27th, 1940. New Spits. arrive with wizard

engines, bags of speed and power, but had to move to "W.M." aerodrome before we could use them on interception patrol.

After a short stay there we had to move to "B.H." on the 8th, which rather "brassed us off," but on arrival we found it quite fun.

November 17th, 1940. This was about my last real do before the end of the blitz period over London.

We were flying at about 15,000 feet when Bob's R/T packed up. I was flying as his number 2 at the time, and as he turned away I followed, and not until I had reached about 10,000 feet did I realise what had happened.

Well! there I was again, all on my own, screwing my neck from side to side as I climbed to rejoin the squadron.

I couldn't tell exactly where they were, so did my best by listening-in on the R/T.

As I got to about 18 or 19 thousand, I heard the controller say over the air that there were about 8 or 9 ME. 109's about and that our boys were to look out. I figured that I must be fairly near both the E/A and our chaps by then, so I looked well around and started a climbing turn to the right and then to the left.

Suddenly, there were tracer bullets whistling past my hood and one or two of the now well-recognised bangs about the aircraft which told me that I had once more been shot-up.

I rolled over and proceeded to spiral down, because I could see it was no good stopping to fight, as my oil pressure was nil. I could see there was oil all over the port main plane as I glided down.

Testing flaps and wheels, I found the latter to work O.K.,

but not the former. I then tried to calculate how long it would take me to reach base, but all of a sudden my engine coughed and stopped. I switched everything off and then looked for a field to land in. I gave a thought to baling-out and then decided that if I put her down in a field, I should most probably save quite a bit of the aircraft.

At about 2,000 feet I spotted a likely field and headed for it, but I wasn't calculating on not having any flaps, so of course I overshot.

Putting my wheels down (very stupid and dangerous) I tried for a field between two long woods running across my nose. I attempted to turn but found that I was travelling much too fast, so in a fit of desperation I yanked up the nose and only just cleared the trees. There in front of me appeared a perfect field, or rather two fields.

I turned to the right and flattened out but she floated for a long time. I then realised how fast I was going, somewhere in the neighbourhood of 140 m.p.h., and also that the field was really in a valley. The machine hit the ground and bounced over the hedge, leaving my port wing in a tree as it went. The wheels were knocked up again (they fortunately failed to lock down), and so when the machine struck the ground again, she slid along the ground on her tummy, the seat broke and I finished up at the bottom of the cockpit. Nothing further happened after that. I extricated myself from the wreckage and got out, rubbing my knees, which were bruised on the dashboard.

After about 15 minutes, some "rustics" took me to the local pub, where I was treated to some beer "before hours." I then rang through to my flight-commander, Pat, who was a Canadian, and had been shot down before, and had only just returned to the squadron. He was very glad to know that I was O.K. – in point of fact, they had only just realised that I was missing about 15 minutes before I rang through. This was a standing joke for a long time afterwards.

Well, that ended my fighting experiences, because the whole squadron was moved to the west of the country for a rest and not much action was seen there.

Editor's Note

Since writing this story Durex has lost his life when baling out after destroying one German machine and driving off two others. The action was fought while defending a convoy of British merchant ships on the North Russian route. The last action of the gallant Durex was to give the position of four German airmen whom he had seen climbing into their dinghy after he had shot down their Junkers 88.

INTRODUCING JIMMY

Jimmy always has a moan but, of course, we all know that it just doesn't mean a thing. He was invariably "brassed off," and was forever telling every one just how "brassed off" he was, but in spite of that he always had a cheerful grin. He's short, well-built, dark-haired with an oval face and high cheekbones, and reminds one of a certain well-known comedian of North Country origin, and is liable to throw something at you if you call him George. He has a great sense of humour, and in his fairly quiet way he often comes out with some gems of remarks, usually in R.A.F. slang. On parties there's no one like Jimmy; as for the booze-wine – beer in his particular case – he can certainly knock it back, and when it comes to nabbling the bogle he is a king pin, an ace in fact.

He is a keen pilot, one of our best section leaders, and although he has been on a vast number of operational trips he didn't have as much luck as some of the other blokes in the way of getting confirmed Huns. However, he's got plenty of time and lots of go left, so here's to his knocking down a few more of the blighters.

Jimmy's Story

When one is asked to recall experience of part of one's flying career, it is not always the excitement of action that flashes to the fore, as many of us do not always get to the blitz areas at the right time, but quite often incidents in training and, perhaps, periods of recreation enjoyed, though perhaps of a doubtful character.

The E.F.T.S. days of doubt, mingled with times of triumph, come readily to mind. Instructors patiently attempting to pump wisdom and the fundamentals of flying into a somewhat scared though eager pupil: the first solo is the common landmark, though strangely enough it slips into the background, and one can hardly recall the forced confidence before, and then the ecstatic feeling of triumph when one walks from the plane a successful first pilot. Perhaps the word "successful" should be replaced, but then again, the old saying goes that any landing from which you can walk away is a good one (though, of course, F.T.S. instructors differ somewhat in their opinions on this statement).

Cross-country flying usually provides many a laugh in E.F.T.S. – some of us get there more by luck than judgment, others "park" anywhere within 30 miles of their destination. Here I would like to say that the good old maxim of "sticking to one's compass" when in doubt is exceptionally sound, and has helped me out of many a fix when I have been too blind to read a map.

I would like to revert, here, to the first solo. As usual, competition was keen to be the first off, and one bright individual who was not at all popular with the boys (one of the "line-shooting" type, conceited, and the perfect example of a human hog) had this honour. His attempt may not have been unique, but it certainly provided plenty of rope with which to pull this unpopular guy's leg. Visibility was not so good for first solo, but fair enough: anyway he made a slight *faux pas* on his circuit, or perhaps he was too clever. He took off from our aerodrome O.K., but did not return; he must have become slightly lost, for he eventually parked down a mere 54 miles away – quite a good effort for a first solo: a budding "Wrong-Way Corrigan" as the boys often reminded him.

During E.F.T.S., there is always the fear of being politely told that you will never make a successful pilot and, in point of fact, that you should never have been born. Many budding pilots were thrown out through sheer inability in flying and others through their lack of brain power in grasping ground subjects. However, at last comes the day when one passes from E.F.T.S. to F.T.S. and hopes run high that you may be posted with your own booze-wine pals. At F.T.S. you strive to get on twin or singles (I was one of the lucky ones), although, of course, there are many fellows who have ambitions for heavy stuff.

Now again comes another first solo, on a service type, in my case a Harvard, a nice steady machine, and a joy for maintenance. After a spell on Harvards, we had a conversion course on to Miles Masters; here we changed from one part of F.T.S. known as I.T.S. to A.T.S., where we did more advanced flying, that is, service flying, air-to-ground and air-to-air gunnery, dive-bombing and bags of formation flying. We had a good crowd of boys in our course, with the four unavoidable "creepers and binders." In A.T.S. I became pally with the "booze-wine boys" who believed in doing things in a baronial style – lashings of wine, food, fruit and girl friends. These expressions may seem a bit batty to the uninitiated, but then, it is often said that only birds and fools fly.

After a very enjoyable F.T.S., came the day of posting to O.T.U. Looking back, I think we were given a very sound training and that my flying had improved along with the development of a very strong head! I have almost forgotten the important day of Wings collection, which occurred half-way through F.T.S., but the only thing I can remember about it was a week-end pass, a slight stir amid congratulations at home and a permissible amount of line-shooting. I might mention here that it is commonly thought in the R.A.F. that along with the Wings goes the collection of beautiful dames, if any, although it has been my experience that the "erks" do far better than the sergeant-pilots. This may be due to the fact that "de girls" shower sympathy on the "erks," or that they imagine that pilots are a low type – a shameful and unjust thought! However, back to F.T.S. and the forthcoming O.T.U., where, here again, comes the suspense, wonder and rumour connected with the particular O.T.U. you were posted to. I was told, for instance, that my O.T.U. had anything from Whitleys to Spits. – this, to a hopeful and eager fighter-pilot, was, to say the least, a little disconcerting.

I remember arriving at the O.T.U. It was raining hard, and I saw rows of Spits. and "Hurri Birds," and I must admit that I breathed a sigh of relief as well as of pleasure. It was here that I missed the luxury of a permanent camp, for we were under canvas and messing was not so good: food "avec grass" and beetles to sleep with. Next morning I met the C.O., and at last was treated as a sergeant for the first time, instead of a "sprogue."

After a trip round the sector in a Master and a dual trip with an instructor to see if we were safe, I was shown the "tits" and gadgets of a Spitfire, and quite simply told that there was nothing to it – the simplest machine to fly, no vices, in fact a baby could fly it. I thanked the instructor, but did not believe him, and with forced confidence strapped myself in, started up and taxied out for take-off. To me it seemed like handling so many pounds of lead on a thread of cotton. I took-off and was at one thousand feet before I realised that I had an "undercart," "pitch to change," and one or two other things to attend to. However, I managed to sort myself out. After about fifteen minutes of stooging around, I agreed with the instructor that a Spitty was the smoothest and lightest aircraft on the controls that I had flown. My landing was not too bad: I remember sinking like a lift and bumping on to the deck, but as the oleo legs did not appear through the top of the wings and I found that it still taxied, I returned to the dispersal.

My stay at O.T.U. was fairly short, but during this time I got in a good many hours on Spits., having become fairly confident on them and passable at formation.

Four of us were posted to the same squadron, and here I experienced some of those annoying but unavoidable moves which are bound to occur in war-time. We were sent to a squadron at "W——" but, on arrival, we found that they had moved, and when we caught up with them at another station, we stayed only one day and were then posted to another squadron, on the east coast – the squadron I am with now. At last I was with a squadron, and we were made comfortable in the mess by one of the sergeant-pilots and, of course, the inevitable question came up, "Are you operational?" We said, "No, but had done a good many hours on Spits." This, apparently, was considered quite good, and we were told that we would be operational in no time. As the squadron was on readiness most of the day, training was difficult to do, but we did some. However, within a fortnight the squadron moved south to "K": we stooges were left behind with one pilot to finish off training. I might mention here that it was August 28th, 1940, and things were happening around London and our kites were soon needed by the squadron, so our training went for a "burton," and we sallied forth to London, eager lambs for the slaughter. But here again we were disappointed. Never shall I forget that Saturday we arrived. London was deserted – a raid alarm but a comparative novelty to us. Driving through London we noticed silvery specks in the sky. A dog-fight was in progress, the fairly distant crump of bombs, with the ear-splitting roaring scream of diving aircraft intermingled with the stutter of machine-guns and the comparative slow cough of the Jerry cannons told their own story. This raid caused a terrific fire amongst the oil tanks at Tilbury. At night the sky was well illuminated, and it was said without undue exaggeration that a paper could be read in Piccadilly that night. This was surely a greeting for budding fighter boys – bags of action. We arrived at the aerodrome to meet the squadron coming back from engaging the forementioned raid. One thing that struck me was one of the boys calmly picking pieces of glass from his reflector sight out of his face, caused by a bullet passing through his hood. It made us think. One incident occurred during the evening of this raid. We were in the local pub crowded with the local lads and females enjoying a steady jug or two. The warning went, and I thought that with the glow of the fire Jerry would have an easy time. Ack-Ack fire became pretty intense and presently crump-crump – a stick of bombs very close, and the last one blew the pub door open. I jumped like hell, and when I turned around the floor was crowded with females and males flat on the floor, and my friend and I were the only people standing at the bar. I must admit I felt terribly embarrassed, but I learned the art of raid procedure. However, the incident enabled me to make a pleasant and profitable acquaintance.

We watched the squadron go up daily to engage terrific Jerry raids, but we were grounded – our too-considerate C.O. considered that we were too raw to fly with the squadron. We filled in our time watching dog-fights and learning squadron procedure, we saw numerous crashes, and had a certain amount of fun going round in a car collecting a few pilots that baled-out. We were disappointed when, after about a week's stay at "K," on September 10th we were posted to a squadron in N.E. England. This squadron had done remarkably well during the early blitz, and practically all the pilots that were left had the D.F.C. or D.F.M. One sergeant had got five Jerries in one day. We were very depressed about this posting, for there was no action up north, although we had a jolly good time with this squadron. We trained and trained with this squadron, formation and more formation, although we were made operational after about three hours' flying. Readiness consisted of standing by, with occasional abortive flaps. My first operational trip was early one morning; dawn was just breaking. We climbed to 15,000 feet to intercept the supposed enemy. I must admit I had a curious feeling in my stomach. The cause of this flap appeared two hours later, when we were ordered off to prevent a Heinkel seaplane from taking-off again after he had "forced lobbed" with engine trouble off the Farne Islands. He was attempting to take off when we arrived but, unfortunately for the Heinkel, there was difficulty in the form of three Spits. Two of the crew were saved. This was a very encouraging start, but the only other interception we had were two Hudsons and a Battle, which were of little use to us. Protective patrols over the shipyards were frequent – damn boring jobs, never any joy, just round and round. The only excitement for me was an engine failure, but a successful "forced lob" was luckily made. Our time was occupied by bags of practice flying, formation, air-to-air gunnery, practice dog-fights and local "stooging" around.

There were quite a few minor pile-ups, but only one serious one in which my friend was a partner. This accident occurred during a practice dog-fight, a head-on collision – one pilot and plane went straight in from about 14,000 feet. The other pilot had a miraculous escape. He remembers a terrific crump, sailing through the air "with the greatest of ease," and then passing out. He next remembers coming to, just above cloud, only to find to his amazement that the parachute was below him or rather that he was hanging base over apex. Further, to add to his dismay and discomfort, he realised he was suspended by one strap only, and that was very insecurely fastened around one leg. Why and how this strap managed to remain fastened is rather a mystery but, fortunately for him, it did. By what must have been a superhuman effort, he pulled himself up and held on to the remainder of the harness, and just before he reached the deck he passed out once more. His only injury was several bruises and a deep cut on his chin caused by his helmet being wrenched off when he was thrown from the cockpit. Of course, he suffered considerably from shock, quite justifiably. His escape was a "one in a million" chance for, when I examined his parachute, two panels were ripped out, the pack ripped to threads, the quick-release box was missing – it had been torn off somehow in company with two of the harness straps, but as previously mentioned, one strap remained intact. It was the strap that passed round the leg through the loop on the pack and up to the quick-release box. When the quick-release box was broken off, this strap must have pulled itself tight round his leg when the buckle caught in the loop and so held him, his weight preventing the strap from slipping. He swears that he never pulled the rip-cord, so when he collided, he must have been thrown out by the force of impact, his chute pack catching on some part of the cockpit and ripping open, and this same force breaking the straps. Of course, accurate information was hard to get, as people after an accident suffer from shock and so are prevented from remembering exactly what happened. If people could have examined the parachute, I am certain that all would have agreed that it was impossible for any one to escape in a parachute so badly damaged. All credit to parachute makers and packers!

Apart from one or two terrific parties in Newcastle, nothing of importance took place up north, but things were still happening down south. As pilots passed off the paybooks or went into hospital for treatment and much-needed rest, others were posted south from training squadrons. Eventually my turn came, and on October 24th I was posted, by good luck, back to — Squadron, who were then operating from "G." Apart from a new C.O. and a few decorations, nothing much had changed in the squadron. They had naturally lost a few pilots, but considering the score they had, the squadron was well up. I hung around for two days, and was then asked if I would like a trip, and I eagerly took my chance. The squadron was ordered up, but we saw nothing. The next day I had the pleasure of watching a dog-fight some 10,000 feet below, but was unable to join in as we were ordered up to 30,000 feet to intercept another raid that was coming in. This raid did not materialise, so a quiet time was had by all! During the next few days the squadron bagged four 109's, but I had no luck.

On November 2nd we moved to "W.M.," where we stayed for about six days only, as the aerodrome was waterlogged. On arriving at "W.M." I had my first crash. We took-off from "G" with the intention of landing at "W.M." after the patrol. I became separated from the squadron, however, and arrived at "W.M." at dusk. I touched-down, ran a few yards, and then I went on a merry-go-round – one oleo leg had gone into a bomb-hole that had been filled in but had sunk badly due to the rain. This leg was left standing upright in the mud to mark the spot, while I spun round in small circles on one wheel and a wing tip; I was shaken but unhurt. However, on November 8th, the squadron moved to "B," the popular home of many fighter squadrons.

At "B" most pilots had a good time in more ways than one – you get good treatment, "dispersals" were comfortable, and, generally, life was made happy. Of course, "B" had been bashed around quite a bit, but that is only to be expected in war-time. At first, we usually took-off for real panics, but before long we started stooge patrols, Maidstone, Tunbridge, Dungeness and Dover at 15,000 to 30,000 feet. November 14th was the last real scrap of the blitz. About twenty 109's and fifty 87's and two squadrons of Spits. took part. Apart from isolated cases, this was the last time Jerry used 87's in any number. It was terribly inconsiderate of him, for the boys liked 87's.

We were up with another squadron from "B." We were leading about 1,000 yards in front and 1,500 feet below. The 87's and escort had just made a rather futile effort of bombing Dover, and were on their way home in fairly decent formation. Our squadron went round in front and the other boys went in behind. Our head-on attack scattered the 87's over the sky, but the other crowd got the pickings, for they bagged twelve 87's and our boys got three and two 109's. However, it was rather hectic while it lasted. About ninety aircraft were scattered all over the sky. Before long, about eight parachutes were descending gracefully towards the sea. Air-gunners in the 87's were apparently quite eager to get out. We did not lose a pilot, but one of the boys had to crash-land at "H."

Apart from one or two chases with high-flying 109's, November held no excitement for me. December and January were very quiet months, but the squadron bagged five 109's during the latter part of November and December. One of them was shot down by my section-leader. Green section were detailed to leave the squadron whilst on patrol, and proceed to Chatham, where a recco-machine was hanging around. A.-A. fire showed us the locality of the bandit, and he was soon spotted, and we were ordered into line astern by the section-leader, who did quick quarter attacks from astern. The pilot of the 109 could not get out of the machine quick enough, for he baled out and finished up in a wood near Canterbury. His plane caught fire and crashed between Chatham and Canterbury. When we arrived back at camp we found that the section-leader had only used twenty rounds from each gun, which, to say the least, was quite a good effort. The weather was pretty bad during December and January, and that probably accounted for the quiet time that we had or, maybe, Jerry had had enough during August, September and October. Anyway, I only did about 12 hours' flying in this time. The only enemy activity during this time consisted of a few recco-machines which were difficult to find in the bad weather, and on most occasions they were intercepted by squadrons stationed on the coast. We had several lectures during December and January on future organisation, fighter sweeps over France, patrols, and many technical lectures. On January 10th, we made the first daylight bombing-raid with fighter escort. Three squadrons of fighters (ours amongst them) swept the Channel off Calais at about 15,000 feet, whilst three more squadrons went in with the Blenheims that knocked hell out of Calais. The A.-A. fire was intense over Calais: we felt the bumps but it was a good way away; the sky was clear, and then hundreds of white puffs appeared that developed into a wall of cloud. Jerry seems to throw all of his stuff up at once. When the bombers had gone home, we left and met no fighter opposition whatsoever.

Things began to liven up in February just a little. We had the usual readiness patrols and interception patrols, but had very little luck. Fighter sweeps were becoming quite fashionable – we did four, but we had no joy. We went over three squadrons strong usually at about 30,000 feet, and it was b——y cold. I had a little excitement on the last fighter sweep we did. Our average height on that sweep was just over 30,000, and the route was Dungeness, Cherbourg, Calais and home. Our squadron was flying in pairs in one large "vic," and we were on our way home and just off Calais when I felt a terrific jolt. I left my seat and black smoke belched from my exhaust, and I thought that I had "bin," but after juggling with the controls and checking the instruments I found that I was quite O.K. However, I was glad when our leader changed direction slightly and increased speed, for the A.-A. fire was too damn close to be comfortable, and considering that we were over 30,000 it was damn good shooting. Jerry had put several bursts below and in the centre of our formation. When we arrived back at "B" we found that three of us had been hit. I had quite a large hole in my rudder and another in the underside of the fuselage.

On February 14th we were sent up on an Interception Patrol, which turned out to be a Channel patrol, and here we met some bad luck. We were top squadron and were patrolling off the French coast around Calais between two cloud layers, when our "weavers" shouted "109's behind." We did a very smart turn about, and I was just in time to see some poor guy who had lagged behind going down with a 109 on his tail and our "weaver" after the 109. They quickly disappeared below the cloud and we collected ourselves together in the hope of seeing the other 109's, but they had disappeared into the cloud. We stooged around, but weather conditions cannot be altered. Two of us became separated from the squadron and we flew around for a bit, and at one time we were about 25 miles inland of the French coast, but we met nothing and so returned, disappointed, to our base. We learned later that our "weaver" had got the 109, but unluckily the 109 had got one of our boys.

Two days later the squadron had somewhat of a revenge when they bumped into a crowd of 109's – unluckily I was not flying and so unable to enjoy the fun. One or two of our boys had their kites shot up, but none were hurt except for one pilot who had a flesh wound in the right arm. The next day my friend had a spot of bad luck. He was jumped by a 109 and stopped a cannon shell in the left arm; he managed a successful crash-landing on Manston by nothing short of superb flying.

On the 24th the squadron moved to "E" for so-called rest, but actually I think the boys would rather have stayed at "B," for at "E" our work consisted of convoy patrols and the very occasional abortive interception patrol. I think fighter-pilots, one and all, agree that convoy work is not a rest but just an infernal bore. Important work, yes, but so damn boring, round and round the same lot of ships for about two hours, quite often three or four times a day and nothing ever seemed to happen. Oh, how we wished for an occasional Heinkel 88 or some other plaything, but no such luck, and all we obtained was bags of flying times. Fifty to sixty hours a month for each pilot throughout the squadron is sure some flying time for single-engine boys. But still, some squadrons have to do this work, and we are one of them, but before long we hope to go back to the London area for a change.

Up to the present, my flying experiences have been far from glorious, and the many-hoped-for victories seem far distant, but perhaps before long I shall be able to acquit myself satisfactorily. All of us cannot be in the midst of the action, for there is work to do on many fields, and the only thing we can do is to execute our duty in the best possible manner wherever one is posted.

INTRODUCING BOGLE

If you think of the "Dead-End Kids" of film fame, imagine one tougher than the rest of them, and you have a good idea of what Bogle looks like. He usually looks somewhat scruffy, and has one of those "fighter-boy" pullovers which he always wears when flying. It is the most torn in the squadron, never has been mended and never will be, and needless to say he's proud of it. He is of medium height with curly hair (not pansy) and a great big smile. There is a certain irresistible charm about him in spite of his rather button nose and tough look. He has far too much energy and whistles constantly, one of his favourite tunes being "Bugle Call Rag."

Bogle was always a difficult bloke at a party. He had a fairly loud voice when he got weaving, a gay laugh, and was a menace with the bogle. He didn't give a damn for anybody even if they were twice his size, and if he took exception he was just as likely to knock them down as argue the point with them.

As a pilot he was magnificent, but on occasions a confounded nuisance, because of his individualistic tendencies. Because of this he was more often than not used as "weaver."

He was awarded the D.F.C. for shooting down the Hun, and could he shoot 'em down! Just read what he says about it!

Bogle's Story

FOR a moment I took my eyes off the leader, and after a quick glance at the surrounding sky gave my instrument panel the once-over: oil pressure and temperature, normal; coolant, um, a bit warm, but we were climbing fast, and it'd soon cool down when we levelled-out. As I looked at the altimeter the needle floated past the 20,000 feet mark. I was glad I'd wrapped up well over my pyjamas.

The three of us had taken-off a few minutes before dawn for the fifth day in succession, in an endeavour to trap a high-flying, early-rising Hun who had been making daily trips to plot the position and course of our merchant convoys. His pals would then come over later in the day in more difficult weather conditions, and bomb the vessels carrying food and produce down our East Coast.

Soon we were on patrol at 25,000 feet. I was number three of our fairly loose formation – loose so that we could devote as much time as possible to searching for our elusive Hun.

I looked back just as the round bulge of East Anglia faded into the mist, but had no idea of the exciting time I was due to have before sitting down to my ham and eggs at base.

Suddenly the well-known voice of our senior ground controller rasped into our headphones, "Hullo, Red I, keep on your present course and height, and you should see him within a minute."

Our three machines seemed to wobble simultaneously as we all hunched forward in our cockpits, and peered around.

Suddenly the leader gave "Tally ho! Yippee! There he is, at 2 o'clock." I looked ahead and a bit to the right, and there he was, a Heinkel III, a few thousand feet below and flying towards us.

He saw us almost simultaneously, and turned, steeply diving away as fast as he could.

I can't remember my thoughts as I sighted my first Hun. I felt a bit sorry for him; he obviously hadn't a chance against three Spitfires. We went in and attacked one after the other. My turn came. I lined up my sights on him, and was far too absorbed in the sight of my tracer bullets vanishing into the fuselage to think about breaking away. I saw the rear gunner's gun flashing and winking at me, but his tracer appeared to be passing by just underneath, so I closed right in and didn't break until almost on the point of collision.

About to attack again, I noticed that my pals were holding back, and then saw the Hun's engines were both stopped, and he was gliding down to land in the North Sea.

The pilot made a nice "pancake" landing on the water, the crew all piled out into a little rubber boat, and the Heinkel slowly sank.

We rejoined formation, and set course for base. I couldn't help thinking of those four fellows back there in the little rubber boat. Suddenly, a few miles from the coast, I began to wonder if I was booked for a dip too.

My engine began to choke and splutter, and twin streams of white smoke issued thinly from my exhaust stubs.

I watched my engine instruments carefully – oil temperature, too high; oil pressure, too low; and all at once everything gave way to one thought – I must reach the coast!

I nursed my faltering engine as carefully as possible, maintaining height with difficulty. Ken and John had pulled to one side, and were "escorting" me in. "I thought you were a bit too close to that rear gunner, old boy," said Ken.

I didn't answer. I was too relieved to see the coast slide back under my wing. Anyway, even if I had to force-land it would be in a field. All fear of splashing around in the icy ocean had gone.

I clattered on and on, watching my tell-tale dials so carefully that I was amazed to find myself almost over the aerodrome. Was I glad to see it?

I put down my wheels and flaps and was at 500 feet, turning into wind to land, when the cockpit filled with clouds of dense smoke. I still had my oxygen mask in position, so hastily turned it on, otherwise I should almost certainly have succumbed to the fumes, which were so thick I couldn't see my instrument panel.

Almost immediately – pouf! my long-suffering engine caught fire, 400 feet from the ground; too low to bale-out, but high enough to provide a few very uncomfortable seconds before landing. I side-slipped vigorously to keep the flames from my face and body, skimmed the branches of a tree, sailed straight through a cluster of telephone wires, and landed on the aerodrome. As soon as I touched-down, the flames became unbearable; I ripped the safety-pin from my harness and dived headlong over the side.

Friends watching my involuntary display swear that the aircraft was doing a good 45 m.p.h. when I left it.

I landed on my face and chest, the tail plane missed me by inches, the aircraft ran straight on, and I sat up in time to see it swing in a huge arc and turn towards me! I was completely winded and quite helpless, but when about sixty yards away the petrol tanks blew up, and the machine collapsed on to its tummy, where it burnt itself out, my unused ammunition popping off merrily, effectively keeping the fire party at a safe distance.

I recovered my wind, and after a cursory examination found that I was quite intact, with no bones broken.

My oxygen mask had saved my face, and my partially inflated "Mae West" had taken a large part of the shock from my chest.

I didn't feel quite so sorry for that rear gunner as I watched my aeroplane blazing away, but my feelings softened again as I sat down to a piled plate of ham and eggs some ten minutes later. After all, he had given me something to "shoot a line about," for to combine one's first Hun and first crash into the same trip is quite an experience.

That little adventure happened on August 8th, and before the end of the month I had seen the end of two more Huns – a Messerschmitt 110 and a Dornier 215.

At that time we were operating from an aerodrome in Norfolk, eating our hearts out for a chance to "go south," where the blitz had just started.

"Up North" our sole action was provided by solitary bombers and reconnaissance planes, usually chased for miles in and out of clouds, whilst we knew that south of the estuary huge formations of bombers and fighters were to be met in a clear sky.

Our dreams were realised only too soon. On September 2nd three of us met our last "lone bomber," another Heinkel, and shot him down, nearly 100 miles out to sea off Great Yarmouth.

When next we took-off, on September 3rd, it was as a squadron, moving to a station a few miles south of London, right in the middle of the "blitz."

I have confused memories of our first few days in the battle of London. Somehow I always became separated from the squadron and gambolled about the sky like a puppy, snapping playfully at huge formations of Jerries, scampering off with my tail between my legs when they turned on me.

Pretty soon I began to settle down. I got used to attacking thirty or forty bombers single-handed, watching ME. 109's closing in on my tail, waiting until the last moment before whirling round in a tight turn to engage them. I had incredible luck in that I always seemed to bump into them, but although I sent several down, knowing they would almost certainly crash, I could seldom confirm them – there were always more to deal with.

Our day was from dawn to dusk, roughly ten hours of whirling dog-fights – flashing tracer-shooting at Huns – being shot at – making new friends – losing old ones – snatching brief naps – the letter home: "Dear Mum and Dad we are still having a very quiet time here . . ." probably written in three sections between patrols! – Some of those letters were never finished – instead, "Mum and Dad" read: "We regret to inform you . . .

Through it all the inevitable radiogram blared forth our favourite tunes unceasingly. Imagine the scene. A dozen youngsters sprawled untidily about a large wooden hut: some asleep, some playing poker, others reading out-of-date *Strands*. Occasionally one would pass a remark considered "punishable" by the rest, whereupon the whole place would be a shambles in a moment – whirling legs and arms, flying cushions – ceasing instantly with the ring of the telephone in the corner. The nearest would answer, "Hallo, patrol base 25,000 feet? Oke."

We'd pile out on to the 'drome, the waiting aircrews would start up our Spits. before we were half-way across to them – on with parachute and helmet, into the cockpit, straps on – "Chocks are away, sir – good luck!" A brief taxi into wind – 12 Spitfires roaring off to come back in two hours' time in ones and twos. Some of us may have packed in during that time the experience of a lifetime.

"O.K. boys, in you go, you know your jobs."

As the leader's voice crackled over the headphones I turned automatically towards the fighters, the 109's, leaving the bombers to the other sections.

I dug my chin into my shoulder and gazed back; my tail was clear, but Joe's – look out, Joe! Look out!

Oh, hell! Why hadn't he looked out?

I throttled back viciously and turned up and over. The bastard who had got Joe couldn't pull up in time. He flashed in front of me, less than 50 yards ahead, my thumb tight on the gun button, it seemed to have been there all my life – all my life bullets had been pouring out of those guns, for Joe.

Now the moment had come. That filthy yellow nose

streaked into my sights, I saw my rounds splashing all along the fuselage, piercing the engine cowlings, shattering his hood. Thick, rolling clouds of black smoke poured from his engine, he rolled over slowly, so slowly, and I followed him – it – down, watching him disappear into a wood, vertically, at 400 m.p.h.

"There you are, Joe, fight it out between you." As I spoke I realised the absurdity of that remark, the stupid bloody-mindedness that had caused it.

My thoughts were cut short. Two more 109's were streaking down hell-for-leather on to my tail. Christ!!!! They saw me do it! they saw me shoot him down! saw him crash, now they are going to kill me for it: but I had to shoot him down; he shot Joe down, didn't he? Joe was my pal, wasn't he?

Terror, stark terror. They were going to kill me. I was at their mercy——

Suddenly I saw tracer flash past. At last here was something I knew, concrete form of the Huns' hatred. I couldn't stop his hatred, but I could dodge his bullets.

Steady, old boy, steady. They've dived from thousands of feet above; must be going twice as fast. I snapped into a steep climbing turn, they were going too fast to follow, and I laughed as I saw them go sailing on by me. I laughed – one's moods change quickly in the air – tension – terror – cool calm action – relief, all in a second.

I turned down after them, throttle blasted wide open. I'd show 'em.

One of them must have lost sight of me; he zoomed up again. Good, I didn't have to waste time chasing him. I cut across the arc of his zoom, stabbed my gun button again –

looked behind. . . . Jeez! was there no end to them! Another was on my tail, coming up fast. I looked in front. My burst had taken effect. He was scampering away, with a steadily increasing cloud of black smoke to keep him company.

Pity I couldn't finish him off, but Carl behind me needed seeing to, and I whirled round, watching his tracer passing beneath me as I drew away from it. But Carl didn't stay to argue. He dived down, and disappeared beneath my wing, and when I had turned again, he had gone. I was alone in the sky.

On the afternoon of Saturday, September 7th, came the biggest daylight raid this country had ever had.

Wave after wave of bombers attacked London from all directions, trying to start fires which would guide their night brothers a few hours later.

It was about 4 p.m. I was washing and shaving, ready for a well-earned "24," when it became evident that the old Hun was going it hot and strong. I threw aside the clean shirt I had been about to put on, and instead donned my dirty old roll-necked pullover and scarf, rushed around to dispersal point and took off to see what I could do. A few minutes later I was over London, at 15,000 feet, with so many enemy formations on each side I didn't know which to go for. From then on I can't piece the story together with any clarity.

I attacked time and again, seldom firing my guns, just slicing through the formations in an effort to split 'em up, doing little or no good. There must have been dozens and dozens of fighters all doing the same thing, all feeling equally lonely.

Suddenly I was surrounded by ME. 109's. I saw one

firing at me from behind; I heard the bullets striking my aircraft; and opened the throttle wide, but there was no response. I turned and dived steeply. They didn't follow. When I was clear I checked-up – oil pressure, zero; oil temp., off the clock. Suddenly my engine seized and the prop stopped dead. Everything was quiet. I was very angry. A few bullets in the wrong places, and I was out of the scrap.

I glided down into the haze, and prepared to make a forced-landing. I was only down to 7,000 feet and had plenty of time. Visibility was shocking. I'd have to wait until the last couple of thousand feet before I selected my landing-field. As I watched for a large field, or even an aerodrome, I automatically took all possible precautions. Straps so tight I couldn't move an inch (better than bouncing about like a pea in a pod and breaking jaws and noses and things); petrol cocks off; ignition off; seat down, in case I turned over, it would save a broken neck at least.

I tried my radio, but it was dead.

Ah, there was a field big enough to land in without damaging the aircraft. I lowered my wheels and flaps, and approached to land. Oh, hell! I might have known. It was full of old motor-cars, blocks of cement, and trip wires to stop enemy aircraft from landing. By now I was down to 800 feet, with no time to pick and choose. I turned away steeply and made for a small stubble field adjoining. As I crossed the hedge a large wood loomed up two hundred yards away. If I landed with my wheels down I'd probably turn over in the soft stubble – a Spitfire isn't a tank. Even if I didn't turn over I'd certainly still be doing 50 or 60 m.p.h. by the time I reached the wood, and could write myself and the aircraft off. There was nothing else for it. I whipped up the undercarriage, and slapped my Spit. down on its belly, only 100 yards from the trees ahead.

There was an almighty jar; the aeroplane went up on its nose – I thought it would turn over. But no, it crashed back. Everything was so still.

I realised I couldn't see. I was in a cloud of smoke. The damn thing must have caught fire after all. I tore off my helmet and straps, jumped out, and ran like hell for yards, with my parachute flapping behind my knees. I sat down abruptly, and turned to watch my blazing aircraft, only to stare amazed at a perfectly sound Spitfire – on its tummy, yes, but otherwise intact, with a cloud of dry earth and dust just settling down around it. So much for my fire scare!

I looked around to see if any one had seen me. No, it was all clear.

Even if they had, I thought, I have every excuse; slowing down from 80 m.p.h. to a standstill in about 2 seconds and as many yards doesn't help clear thinking.

I got up and walked to the aircraft. I picked up my helmet. It was covered in light-brown dust, and I realised that I was covered from head to foot in dry earth. I looked at the damage. I had only been hit by about a dozen bullets, but two or three of 'em had hit the oil system in the wrong place, and that accounted for my engine failure. Two men came running wildly across the field. They stopped, panting, and looked a little self-conscious. "All right, chum?" said one. I reassured them, and asked my way to the nearest telephone. They showed me and I walked to a farm-house, where a man and his wife and a sweet little kiddie did all they could for me. I hoped they didn't think I was rude, for I was in such a hurry to get away. I wanted to get back to the aerodrome and take-off again. I soon realised it was hopeless. It was 5.15 p.m., I'd never be back before dark. I couldn't get through to my base, so phoned the nearest aerodrome, and gave them particulars. They promised to let my squadron know, but they never did, and the next day I was posted as missing.

A policeman arrived, fat and perspiring, in a small car. He seemed excited; when I got to the car I saw why. He had a mixed bag, for my travelling companion was a blond youth, quite handsome, and very pleasant, but a Nazi!

We introduced ourselves, and took quite a liking to each other. We held a long conversation in the police station. He had been shot down by a Spitfire, and had baled-out of his 109. We laughingly agreed that the honours were even in our two cases!

He had been particularly unfortunate, for he had received the Iron Cross that very morning.

He was 23, and unmarried. Very grateful for the bar of chocolate I gave him. We exchanged buttons and badges and addresses. I still have his little badge and address in my wallet. We would write, "after the war."

Soon I had to leave him. A policeman took me on the next stage of my journey back to base. An Irishman, he drove at a great rate, usually on the wrong side of the road. He dropped me in a village at 8 p.m., and I spent the night there, getting transport from the local aerodrome in the morning.

I arrived back at base in the afternoon. The squadron had received no news of me, and I was given up for dead.

My people had been told I was missing. I soon put that right!

Imagine the party we had that evening; interrupted by the news at 9 o'clock. The announcer's voice came over loud and clear, "One of our pilots previously reported missing has since returned safely to his unit."

The drinks were on me.

The morning of September 15th dawned – blue, cloudless sky, fine flying weather.

It was Sunday – what of it? Hundreds of bombers and fighters swarmed over the Channel.

Our turn didn't come until about half-past eleven, when we were ordered to patrol at 20,000 feet; off we went.

I was in my usual position as "weaver," flying alone 1,000 feet above the rest of the squadron, watching for attack from the rear, or out of the sun.

Soon we spotted a formation of Dorniers, and the squadron attacked. I followed, keeping a keen look-out behind, and wasn't surprised to see a dozen or more 109's diving down on us.

By now the foremost people in the squadron were in amongst the Dorniers, so I told 'em about the 109's, and engaged the nearest, but before I could get him in my sights I was fairly in the soup; they were all round me.

They didn't do their job and protect the bombers, but all went for me, because I was on my own. I saw the squadron disappearing, dealing most effectively with the fleeing Dorniers, and realised that I was in no position to stay and play with a dozen 109's. Several were on my tail, so I beat it, straight down, flat out. I levelled out at 12,000 feet; that had shaken 'em off. I was all alone. I called up the squadron on the radio, told 'em I was no longer with them, and beetled off to see what I could find, patrolling a few miles south of London.

I saw a blob coming up from the south, and investigated. Boy! oh, boy! Twenty fat Dorniers, flying wing-tip to wing-tip, Ack-Ack all round.

I was well ahead and above them, so shoved the old throttle open, and dived at them head on.

I picked the chappie who appeared to be leading the bunch, settled him in my sights, and let him have it.

There isn't much time to muck about in a head-on attack. I gave a short burst, then slid underneath his big black belly with only feet to spare, and flashed through the rest of the formation. I hadn't meant to cut it so close, and instinctively ducked as I saw wings, engines, cockpits and black crosses go streaking past my hood.

I had reached about 450 m.p.h. in my dive, and heaved back on the stick. I "blacked-out" completely as I went up and over in an enormous loop. My sight returned as I lost speed and the centrifugal force lessened. I was on my back, so rolled over. The speed of dive and pull-out had carried me up ahead of them for another attack.

I saw that my first burst had taken effect, the leader had dropped away and to one side, and was turning back. The rest of the formation were wobbling about, and didn't seem to know quite what to do.

As I dived down again, two Hurricanes turned up and joined in the party.

The Huns didn't wait for more, but scattered and fled pell-mell, jettisoning their bombs on open country.

I had helped turn 20 bombers away from London! I

yelled and whistled with joy, then pounced on the one I had crippled in my first attack. The Hurricanes were "seeing off" the others O.K., so I left them to it.

He appeared to be having difficulty with one engine. I fixed that by stopping it altogether for him. He looked a bit lopsided then, so I stopped the other one too, and he started a long steep glide down.

I saw the rear gunner bale-out, so went up very close and had a look at the aeroplane. It was pretty well riddled. Eight machine-guns certainly make a mess!

I had a look at the pilot. He sat bolt upright in his seat, and was either dead or wounded, for he didn't even turn his head to look at me, or watch out for a place to land, but stared straight ahead.

Suddenly a pair of legs appeared, dangling from the underneath hatch. The other gunner was baling-out. He got out as far as his waist, then the legs kicked. They became still for a moment then wriggled again, they writhed, thrashed and squirmed. Good God, he's stuck! Poor devil, he couldn't get in or out, and his legs, all I could see of them, flailed about wildly as he tried to release himself.

It was my fault, I suddenly felt guilty, and almost physically sick, until I thought of the people down below, wives, young mothers, kiddies, huddied in their shelters, waiting for the "All Clear."

The legs still wriggled and thrashed, 2,000 feet above the cool green fields, trapped in a doomed aircraft, gliding down, a dead pilot at the controls.

First one boot came off, then the other. He had no socks on, his feet were quite bare: it was very pathetic.

He'd better hurry, or it'd be too late.

He hadn't got out before they were down to a thousand feet. He'd be cut in half when they hit the ground, like cheese on a grater. In spite of all he stood for, he didn't deserve a death like that. I got my sights squarely on where his body would be, and pressed the button. The legs were still.

The machine went on. The pilot *was* dead. He made no attempt to flatten out and land, but went smack into a field, and the aeroplane exploded. I saw pieces sail past me as I flew low overhead. I didn't feel particularly jubilant.

After a hasty lunch we were back on patrol, and soon ran into loads of bombers.

ME. 109's were escorting them high above, but they didn't interfere when we attacked.

I picked out a Dornier 17 at 1,000 feet below, and dived at him head-on, my favourite way of dealing with bombers. He went into a steep dive and I followed, firing as I caught up to him. The rear gunner returned my fire for a moment, and I felt something hit my foot. I found afterwards that it was a spent bullet which had passed through part of my engine, it didn't even go through my flying boot.

Then the return fire stopped. The gunner must have ducked behind his armour plating, or I may have got him, for as I overtook them, and slid by under the left wing, there was no sign of him and his gun was swinging idly on its mounting.

We went into cloud at about 5,000 feet. I followed. It was only a thin layer, and as he passed through, one of the crew baled-out O.K.

The dive grew steeper as it plunged earthwards. Then,

wham! it smacked into a wood, and blew up, burning fiercely, setting fire to some of the trees.

I climbed again. After about ten minutes, saw two more Dorniers, well below me, flying along together in very tight formation, wings overlapping.

Good, I was ahead of them, and down I went in the good old head-on dive, and it got results!

They seemed surprised to see me, for they wobbled and separated so violently that their wings touched, and a chunk came off one wing-tip. They both lost height, and I gave them a quick burst each for luck. One was almost on his back as he went into the cloud-layer, the other seemed to be out of control too.

I followed them through. We were now just off our coast.

The first went headlong into the "drink," there was an almighty splash, and he disappeared.

The second was spinning. A piece off one wing, he spiralled crazily down into the water. It reminded me of chestnut leaves in the autumn, fluttering down on to the school playing field. He hit, exploded, and petrol and oil burned fiercely on the surface of the sea. The flames died away, only a few bits of wreckage remained floating.

I remembered seeing another Dornier explode, and burn – let me see, when was it? Why, only that very morning. It was still Sunday, September 15th. The day had been a year.

I flew to the coast, and set course for home.

Passing low over fields and villages, rivers and towns, I looked down at labourers working, children at play, beside a big red-brick schoolhouse, a bomb crater two streets away; little black heads in the streets, turning to white blobs as they heard my engine and looked up.

I thought of workers in shops and factories, of stretcher-parties and A.R.P. wardens. I hoped the "All Clear" had gone. I was tired, I'd done my best for them.

Editor's Note

Since these lines were written we learn with very great regret that Bogle has been killed in a flying accident. What a waste it all seems!

INTRODUCING BOB

Bob is a tallish, good-looking, fair-haired bloke with very typical schoolboy complexion and features, liable to blush every now and then; very much the Englishman in conversation and manner. He has a funny way when talking to you over a beer of hopping stiff-leggedly from one foot to another – all very strange but really very nice. Being a little shy it took one some time to get to know him really well, but when the barriers had been broken down he blossomed into what one might almost call a carefree youth of some 23 years of age.

He is an excellent flight-commander, and as a pilot was much above the average. His keenness for the welfare of the squadron, apart from the normal duties of a flight-commander, was greatly added to as, by sheer chance, he was posted to the squadron, and to the particular flight which his father had commanded during the last war.

For his very good work as a flight-commander and the number of Huns which were confirmed against his bag he was awarded, and very well deserved, the D.F.C.

Bob's Story

3 P.M. one afternoon in April, 1939, some ten or so pilots were strewn around the crew-room adopting the most comfortable attitude they could in the somewhat dilapidated bits of furniture which were known to R.A.F. stores as "chairs, Mark 3, lounge, pilots, for the use of." A few talking, most of them dozing, one conscientiously struggling to get his flying log book up-to-date at the one table which the rather dingy room boasted. All were waiting for 4.30 p.m., which time told them they had earned their respective rates of pay and that tea and toast was ready in the mess.

No one seemed to notice an orderly-room clerk arrive, quietly deposit a sheaf of typewritten papers on the table, and just as quietly disappear. A minute or so later Tim looked up from his log book and through a haze of mental arithmetic suddenly got the meaning of those inoffensive papers.

"Night flying." Tim's anything but quiet voice shattered the room. Pilots and squadron dogs alike sat up and took notice. Copies of night-flying orders were grabbed and excited voices babbled. Snatches of conversation could be discerned giving no idea of the general opinion. "Damn, had a bloody good date tonight." "Weather looks pretty punk." "Bet Dicky will be 'browned-off' when he knows," and so on.

Flying kit was collected together, daily inspections

carried out, night flying tests carried out, flare path laid, and some 12 pilots were ready to "dice with death" that night. It was only the second time the squadron had flown Spitfires at night, hence the somewhat tense excitement; the wooden-bladed Spitties' virtues and vices at night had yet to be discovered. But in spite of these little worries Tim's two words heralded what was to prove the most eventful few hours of night-flying in the squadron's history, particularly for yours truly.

At approximately 22.30 hours, my allotted time, I sped along the flare path and staggered into the air in the wake of four others. Three of them were doing formation practice, the fourth chap and I stooging around the sector for an hour. It was a gorgeous night, full brilliant moon, stars, tremendous visibility, and all the street-lit towns looking like fairyland. Several others had taken-off after me, and altogether there were nine aircraft up.

I made for London, and after some time managed to make out Piccadilly, Oxford Street and the rest. Life was well worth living, but I still kept a good weather eye on the flashing red beacon which told me where the aerodrome was. After looking around for a time I looked at the clock and decided it was time to return to the aerodrome and take my place in the circuit.

About thirty miles from home the friendly beacon disappeared, and in spite of straining my eyes I could not see it any more. I flew on the course back and soon found I was over a little town not more than seven miles from the aerodrome. From this point I noticed with horror that low cloud had formed and stretched from this little town to the north as far as I could see. Jimmy, who had been leading the first formation, had just landed with his boys and had noticed this cloud forming. He called up on the wireless and told all aircraft to land immediately, whereupon we told him we could not see the aerodrome. We flew over the top of the cloud, which was at 1,000 feet, and the base, Jimmy said, was 200 feet. Rockets were sent up through the clouds to indicate the position of the aerodrome beneath. After the second rocket I saw a second formation with Patrick leading, and an odd aircraft which I knew was Duggie.

I was instructed to come down and land, so I gently sank through the clouds 400—300—200 feet, then I burst through, sweating somewhat freely, and finding myself over some village church. I yelled for more rockets, and one was fired. Luckily I saw it and found the aerodrome with a sigh of relief.

At this point I heard instructions being given to the boys still above the clouds to proceed south to another aerodrome where it was clear of cloud. Duggie had already found a 'drome east of us. The story goes that he found himself on a bomber aerodrome and went in the Watch Office to look at Daily Routine Orders for the station to find out where he was.

As I flashed round the aerodrome at the colossal altitude of 800 feet I found that there seemed to be precious little light on the aerodrome. I afterwards found that Sergeant "W.," who had landed some ten to fifteen minutes earlier, had hit the floodlight on landing and had written-off both it and his aircraft, but was unhurt. Thinking, "Well, it's now or never," I put down the wheels and flaps, made a long, low, flat and fast approach and eventually touched-down half-way along the flare path still going quite fast. I knew I couldn't take-off again with a wooden fixed airscrew and didn't want to much either. Consequently I made for a corner of the aerodrome in order to get a longer run, crossed the flare path, and then saw a fence looming up. I closed my eyes, braced myself and prayed, waiting for the inevitable awful things to happen. But they didn't. There was first a bump like a bad landing, and the aircraft came to rest still right way up. So I turned off the petrol, ran the carburettor dry, and switched off. Climbing out, I realised that I had gone through a hedge, over a main road, bounced over a ditch, through another hedge, and into a muddy field behind the officer's married quarters. Meanwhile consternation reigned on the other side of the road. Fire-tender and "blood waggon" were chasing up and down the road, along with Jimmie on a bicycle. Nothing actually could be seen in the dark as the aircraft wheels had left only two small holes as they passed through the brush fence. The old Spittie was taken back along the main road and in through the gate past the guardroom – the only way back to the aerodrome! The total damage turned out to be two dents of about an inch in the undercarriage fairings and some twigs in the oil cooler.

* * *

Even though a telegram recalled me after only two days' leave of my allotted seven, I wasn't disappointed as I had to rejoin my squadron in the South where it had moved in my absence. Action at last!

When I saw the boys I had quite a shock. They looked quite tired, and some of them were wounded, with burns and splinters. Three chaps had baled-out, two had been killed, but it was not without leaving a mark. The squadron's score had been just about doubled. I discovered that I had a new flight-commander in Pat, but he'd the misfortune to get shot-up and burnt before baling-out, so I took over the flight.

During that evening on which I returned to the squadron early in September, Ken, the "A" flight-commander, in answer to my questions, said, "Don't do too much first time; just keep your eyes open, see what goes on, and watch your tail, until you get something worth shooting at."

The Huns had been coming over in large raids, almost clocklike, three times a day – after breakfast – at noon – and finally at about tea-time. Up we went the following morning and after a short patrol enemy aircraft were sighted. We flew towards them and as we neared them a dread cry burst on our ears from somebody, "Look out, 109's attacking."

I looked around and couldn't see anything very near, but the squadron was splitting up and going hell-for-leather towards the bombers. Suddenly a flaming object which I recognised as an ME. 109, blazing from wing-tip to wing-tip, flashed down a hundred yards in front of my nose. This shook me not a little, and from that point the sky seemed black with aircraft. Yet I seemed very much alone, the twisting, turning aircraft all around seemed to my unaccustomed eyes to be all Jerry's, though in actual fact, of course, they weren't. I then recognised a Heinkel toddling along a bit above me some six or seven hundred yards away.

Off I went after him, out for the kill so to speak, when

Ken's words came to me. I whipped round to have a look-see at my tail, and sure enough there was a nasty-minded 109 getting precious close, diving from above. From that position I didn't stay to argue, but went bowling down in the hammest manner possible. On recovery I found I was too far away to get back to the fight, having lost so much height, but it taught me the valuable lesson of "look before you leap!"

In the following patrol during the afternoon I had a couple of pots but knew I hadn't hit anything. The following afternoon, however, we again intercepted, and I succeeded in squirting a couple of Heinkels, but I was attacked by 109's and dived away. As we were near the coast I looked around for anything odd trying to get home to North France. I was delighted to find a Dornier 215 just crossing the coast below me at about 9,000 feet. Sailing in, I gave the fuselage a burst just in case there might be a rear gunner there to stop some lead and incidentally stop him giving me any. Then, sitting on his tail, I belted the Dornier's starboard engine. It burst into flames. By now the E/A was diving quite fast for some clouds beneath. I gave the port engine the rest of my ammunition and the E/A went into cloud.

Noticing smoky streaks passing my starboard wing, I looked in my mirror, and saw a 109 attacking, so having no "ammo" left and being in a nasty position, I, too, faded into cloud – straight down. Some 2,000 feet lower I burst through just out to sea off the coast. As I straightened out I noticed a glow in the cloud nearby and the 215 came tearing through, diving almost vertically with both engines alight. Smacking the water about six miles from the coast, he disappeared. My previous score being one-third Heinkel, I now had drawn one complete tooth from Jerry's Luftwaffe, and returned to the aerodrome greatly elated. Life wasn't too bad after all.

September 15th, 1940. The grandest day in the history of the Royal Air Force; the day when the Luftwaffe sent over its mightiest raids on London, and were turned back, finishing the day with 185 German aircraft on English soil and in the Channel. To crown it all, Bomber Command and Coastal Command had a night out blitzing the invasion ports.

We also had a good day, or rather a good afternoon. It wasn't until this time that we got mixed up in the biggest raid of the lot. All the aircraft which fell to our guns, definite, probable and damaged, were bombers, so we had great cause to feel we had done something.

On this particular raid I'm practically certain we were the first squadron to intercept, and being the leader of the look-out section I was responsible for us trying to ward off the ME. 109 escort-fighters from the other boys. However, we weren't attacked, and as I looked round again I saw the rest of the squadron slap in amongst the bombers, breaking several away from the formation.

Floating round, I found a Heinkel III getting a hell of a plastering by four or five Hurricanes and Spits., so I gave it a squirt for luck just before he went into cloud. When last I saw him his wheels had come down, and he was looking awful sick. My number 3 followed him through the "cotton wool" and along with several of the other fighter boys wasping around. He told me afterwards that they succeeded in making the Jerry crash on a nearby aerodrome.

Meanwhile I was still above cloud and slap underneath all the fireworks. There must have been well over 300 Nazis, and I don't think one British squadron missed action that day. One gets the idea that there were one or two aircraft knocking about.

Climbing up to the mix-up I was attacked by a 109. Luckily I saw him start his attack, so I waited as long as I dared and then whipped around. This latter manœuvre had two reasons for its execution – firstly, to get out of the way, and secondly, with a vague idea of getting on the 109's tail in the process. However, he was going far too bloody fast and I couldn't catch him. He went into cloud and I followed, hoping to get him underneath, but the cotton-wool was very thick, and when I came out he was nowhere to be seen.

Knowing then that I was out of the fight, I started back home, tooling along at only 2,000 feet. It was then I saw some anti-aircraft bursts, so I turned, and saw a Dornier 17 plumb in the middle of the "flak," climbing towards the cloud. I could scarcely believe my eyes and good fortune, and I also thought it queer that he was going North. However, yours truly didn't stop to argue but sailed in on the port side and saw my bullets going home. As I broke away from this attack I saw two of the crew bale-out. I went again to attack in exactly the same way from the other side, and this resulted in the pilot and another getting out. The old "Flying Pencil" went spiralling down and crashed in a back garden in Rochester.

I believe fate must have sent me that Dornier, because several other fighters were knocking around, but none of them seemed to have seen it. That is, of course, with the exception of my C.O., who was about 1,000 feet below me when I made my attacks. The "17" was going down before he got up to it.

The boys came home in ones, each with a terrific tale, and usually a Hun. A grand day for the squadron with not one pilot hurt in any way.

One evening, three days later, we were up as part of a two-squadron wing on patrol, and happened to run into a bunch of 109's at almost the same height. There was a funny sort of mist about at this altitude, and I did not see the bunch of bombers which these ME.s were escorting. However, our co-squadron dealt with the bombers, and as we swept off to attack the 109's they climbed for the mist. Ken, who was leading the squadron, chased one. I was leading the second section, and when the squadron began to split up I followed Ken but couldn't keep up with him, so I went after another.

Dizzy, my number two, kept with me, so I knew my tail was O.K. I climbed from behind and beneath the 109. Eventually I was about in range and saw that he obviously had not seen me, so, holding my fire, I crept right in, giving two bursts from just behind him. The first knocked bits off him, and the second sent some incendiaries into his petrol tank. Up in flames went the whole issue and the pilot baled-out pretty darned quick.

I stalled and dived away. Dizzy, the old bloodhound, kept with me, and we saw nothing else. Even the bombers had disappeared. Coming down to 15,000 feet we noticed some ack-ack bursts going out to sea. As we watched, the flak came in again and then stopped.

Shortly afterwards we saw about four fighters fading in and out of the haze. Dizzy yells out, "It's O.K., Bob, they're friendly," to which I replied, "I'm not so sure."

Up we climbed round the haze, and saw them come out of this about 200 feet above us. I was right, they were ME. 109's, so in we sailed, guns belching. They broke into pairs, two going over me and tackling Dizzy, and I went for the others. My two broke up, one diving down. I got a lovely sight on him and hell, I had left the button on "Safe." However, I put it on "Fire" pretty quick, getting a squirt in at the 109. I saw lumps of things fly off him, including one of the famous 109 tailplane struts. I also noticed tracer coming past me from behind.

I didn't need to ask what that meant, so yours truly blacked-out in the hammest turn over. Still, it was effective. After that I had no idea where everything was or where Dizzy had got to. I could see no sign of my winged bird, and didn't know whether he had been able to get back home.

Five minutes after landing I was relieved to see Dizzy on the circuit. He landed and said he'd got one of his 109's in flames. Shortly afterwards we were released for the day, and we went off to have the odd noggin in celebration of what we, anyway, called a successful day.

I think I can honestly say that October 25th provided the most exciting hour of my young life.

We were sent off on our usual "after breakfast" patrol, hiccoughing away with that awful mixture of a hastily swallowed fried egg and oxygen. After tooling around for nearly an hour at over 30,000 feet, the squadron sighted flak bursts at our own height on our starboard side.

The enemy aircraft were then seen below us, and were recognised as ME. 109's. They were travelling in approximately the opposite direction, and we for once were in that lovely position above and in the sun. We came down and into the attack, and it was a case of take your pick. I picked one.

He must have received some warning, however, because before I could get in range, he went tearing straight down. The 109 has some good points, and diving is definitely the best. I followed him and found that we were going vertically down.

With almost pathetic slowness I was overtaking him, holding my fire until I was in range. We had gone down so quickly, and were attaining such an incredible velocity, that I was almost certain we were quite out of the rest of the dog-fight, and that no other nasty-minded Jerry would interfere with me. I was wrong. Very wrong.

Having just got into range of my target, I was literally just about to press the old tit when there was a hell of a crash and thump on my aircraft. It was the unmistakable heralding of a cannon shell, and I counted five more in quick succession. Owing to the high speed I couldn't take very quick evasive action, and in any case I soon found that I had no elevator-control at all. The 109's pal had definitely got me.

The aircraft went into a steep left-hand climbing turn, and for a little while afterwards that was all I saw. Owing to the colossal pressure I just blacked-out completely. I tried to lift my hands to open the hood, but I couldn't. I put the stick in every position, but for all I know it had absolutely no effect.

It seemed an age. The engine seemed to howl more and more, and then, seems funny, I gave in, thinking, "Hell, and I'd nearly got him; well, it's been a grand life; bit short though; wish it would hurry up and hit; can't bear the suspense."

The pressure eased off, my eyes told that; the black-out wasn't so dense; my one prayer was that I should come to looking at blue sky and not mother earth, 'cause then I'd be going up and not down. There we are – yes, blue sky – relief number one.

Two gauntletted hands literally flew to the hood release and tugged, no result; tugged again, same thing; one bloody great wrench and she flew open. Relief number two. Flames from the oil tank were bouncing about in the corner of the cockpit, and spurred me to greater efforts.

Off came the Sutton harness release ring; I stood up. Blast! I'd forgotten my helmet, and was still fastened to the aircraft – ducking back out of the slipstream I actually tore the helmet leather as I wrenched it off. (I found the helmet afterwards and was amazed at the strength I must have used to tear it like that.) Into the slipstream, again leaning slightly to the left, and, hey presto, the wind had plucked me out – relief number three.

"Cor bleeding 'ell." My impressions and thoughts in one. A delightfully fresh breeze as I dropped through space cooled my face and ears. About time to pull the old string. Take it easy – don't fumble – hands seem frozen – where's that blasted ring? – got it! A sharp pull and a jerk – parachute open – relief number four.

But how had it opened? Not properly; my left foot was caught up in the silk cords and I was upside down. Knowing that it wouldn't be the nicest way to contact Kent, I climbed up the other side of the parachute, hand over hand, and after a short struggle, managed to free my foot. Relief number five.

Dropping into more or less the "right way up" position, became conscious of the quietness of everything; the only sound being the spasmodic rattle of machine-gun fire, and howl of engines, in the battle still going on far overhead, and also the large wheezing semi-choking noises coming from me as I gulped in air for the first time since, it seemed, we started the attack on the Huns. Looking around I realised that the 'chute wasn't properly open. The shoulder-straps, instead of holding me behind the shoulder-blades, were tangled together, chafing my ears. Farther up some of the silk cords were crossed, and I realised that the silk canopy was not so fully open as it should have been. Consequently, I was failing considerably faster than I should have been. Struggle as I might, I could not improve the position. A glance at my wrist-watch – 9.25 – wonder what time I'll hit – a cloud beneath – do a practice landing on it to see just how fast I'm going. Judging by the rate at which I passed that cloud I was going pretty fast. It fairly whizzed past. I afterwards discovered that this was at 7,000 feet, and I reckon I couldn't have been less than 27,000 feet when I was shot-up. I guess I got out at about 11,000 feet, so I must have dropped about 16,000 feet blacked-out. No wonder it seemed an age.

Floating down in this somewhat uncomfortable position, I saw a town beneath me, and just prayed I should land in a tree to break my fall. Gradually I drifted south-westish, occasionally breaking into a swing and twisting slowly round.

Soon I had the impression that I was falling as I got lower, and not that I was stationary in mid-air.

I tried to judge whereabout I should "kiss the floor" again, but trees seemed far away. Lower and lower, over a farm-house, in which I saw curious faces looking skywards. Down to about 500 feet and over some high-tension cables, which, even though I was several hundred feet above them, made me instinctively lift my feet up. Lucky me! I saw I was going to land in not just a tree, but a whole wood. Relief number six.

Just above the topmost branches I covered my face with my arms to prevent getting branches in my eyes. There was a breaking of twigs and I looked around to find myself bouncing up and down between a couple of trees like a human yo-yo. The canopy had caught in the interlocking branches of the two trees, and I was in mid-air. Those trees were tall. They were of the type with no lower branches to catch hold of. Twenty feet up and almost over an asphalt road, so I couldn't release the harness and drop without fear of injury.

I discovered a small twig sticking out from one of the trees out of reach. So then I did a Tarzan stunt, swinging back and forth until I got enough momentum to catch the twig. Gingerly pulling myself in, praying it wouldn't break, I reached the trunk, scrambled up into the branches, released the harness and lay there panting.

Farmers, housewives, errand boys and Home Guard all arrived at once on the road beneath, doubting my nationality, but my language seemed to convince them I couldn't be other than British. The Home Guard gallantly made a human ladder to me, sitting on each other's shoulders, and a minute or so later I touched the earth. I felt sick, and was rescued by a squadron-leader, who had followed me floating down, in his car. He produced the odd noggin of brandy, and as I was borne away to a hospital for the once-over I felt my real self for the first time for a good twenty-five minutes. Final relief.

INTRODUCING MAX

Max was only with the squadron a very short time and he is one of those who have contributed to this book who have been posted as "missing." He didn't even finish the story before that last trip from which he failed to come back. Max was a tremendous fellow, medium height and heavily built. He had massive shoulders, a bull neck, and gave the impression of being some six foot round the chest. He was extremely keen on wrestling and boxing, at both of which sports he was very proficient.

Max was rather quiet, shy and softly-spoken, with little to say but lots of sense when he did speak. I think he was very much an Idealist. That last patrol came before we really had a chance to get to know him very well. I think without exception he was extremely well liked and was lots of fun at the one or two parties which we were on together.

Max's Story

DURING the year 1938 Germany invaded Czechoslovakia. This caused a major crisis in Europe in which Britain was immersed. The majority of the British population then realised that we should have to be fortified in case Herr Hitler gave the world twenty-four hours to clear out.

Often I have been thrilled by the stories of men who had fought in aerial combat in the Great War. It then became my sole ambition to put fiction into reality and emulate their success in the war which I felt must come in the near future. In order to accomplish this it was essential to start flying without any loss of valuable time, and the opportunities of the R.A.F. Volunteer Reserve strongly appealed to me and provided the chance to realise this burning desire.

The darkening storm materialised at last – what seemed inevitable became a reality in September, 1939, when war was declared.

Till then my experience had been elementary, so that my chance of immediate action seemed small. Fortunately things did not warm up until I was fully trained and fit for the front line in combat. It was during this period of training I saw for the first time a real Hun plane with the conspicuous black crosses on wings and fuselage. I was at a great disadvantage, being well out in the open and right on its target.

The plane was a JU. 88. It came out of the low cloud in a roaring dive: machine-guns were blazing from the gun turrets. I threw myself flat on the ground, bullets were whistling close, too close to be comfortable, and then came the siren-like sound of bombs. I thought this was the end, but, thank God, the German pilot, though coming low, overshot his target and spoiled the whole attack. There was a lull and I looked up to see where he was. Still there right enough and turning round to come in again to blaze away with machine-guns. This was his last effort, for as if by magic, three Spitfires appeared on the scene and I saw, for the first time, an aerial combat. It was just a matter of seconds before the German crew were roasting in their bullet-riddled plane. This was no sooner over when another appeared and to our great delight he hit the dust in the same manner.

This little episode made me very bloodthirsty and I longed for the time when I should take part in the fray. The whole thing seemed just too easy! It was later I found out my mistake.

After many weeks of practice dog-fights and aerobatics I was sent to an operational training unit, where I gained experience on the world's fastest and most beautiful aeroplane – the Spitfire. The Spitfire has exceeded all expectations; she is a real thoroughbred.

In a short time my friend Peter and I were posted to a fighter squadron in the East of England, where we gained valuable experience in squadron formation. The Hun did not trouble us much at that sector and our squadron moved to a more advantageous position on the west side of the country, where he was becoming a positive nuisance.

I was thrilled when I looked down on the country over which I had done the greater part of my training. I felt that, having learned to fly a Spitfire, I had accomplished something. Peter and I were only too pleased to show off in daring flight over our old aerodrome, at times to the annoyance of instructors.

We did many patrols over the Irish Sea without any success, but one night we were notified that seven Dornier bombers were steering a course that would bring them directly on our patrol line. They arrived at sunset. For many of them it was the last time they would see the sun disappear over the horizon. Every one of them was shot down without ever reaching their target. It was a good fight with a grand finish.

At this time London was being turned into a living hell by incessant bombing. Peter and I were posted to a new squadron in the London area – a Scottish squadron. Being a Scotsman myself, I was proud to be allied with such men. They had done some splendid service.

We arrived late one afternoon and were deeply interested in listening to the thrilling tales of some of that day's combats with the enemy. There was plenty of activity and Peter and I knew that our skill would soon be tested. We were not unduly worried at the prospect of imminent conflict; we knew that the Hun did not like Spitfires. And we remembered also, the true words of the Squadron-Leader, a famous pilot of the last war who was credited with seventy-five victories, that the Hun was much more scared than you when fighting. If so, he must have been damned scared at times.

After a good night's rest we were all set and ready for a fight. The squadron was called to readiness at dawn. After testing our pressures and oxygen and placing helmet and parachute in the planes all ready for a quick take-off, we adjourned to the dispersal hut where we awaited the voice of the operator over the "tannoy" to tell us to take-off. We had not long to wait. The order came and we ran like hell for our planes. My excitement was great as the mechanics were helping me into my harness and strapping me in. At one point I thought I heard machine-gun fire – only imagination, or it may have been my knees knocking. In a short time our Merlin engines burst into life and seemed itching to get off the ground and into action.

The squadron looked like a swarm of wasps as they taxied out for the take-off, and what a sting they had, but it was not in the tail. It was only a matter of minutes before we looked down on old Father Thames from a height of thirty thousand feet; if we could prevent it no Hun would cast a shadow over our little Danube. From the controller in the operations room we were informed that there were three or four raids coming in of about thirty fighter bombers each, and along different parts of the South-East coast. To my relief we learned that we were not the only squadron waiting for them. We were detailed for the raid that was making for our part of the sector.

From the Radio Transmission every pilot knows exactly what is happening, and with the knowledge that we were getting nearer and nearer to the Huns the feeling became more intense. I kept looking to see if my firing button was on "Fire," my reflector sight switched on, and plenty of oxygen. I was all eyes and ears for information of our approaching enemies. Far ahead we could see the smoke trails of about thirty ME. 109's. To me they looked a greater number, however. At such times one is apt to suffer from a little imagination. They were about 2,000 feet above us and appeared to be climbing like dingbats. We had all tits pressed and were almost hanging on our props to gain the advantage of height, which in combat is the main thing. In this we did not quite succeed. They crossed just above us in very close formation; the black crosses were visible and seemed to fascinate me. They were now very close. I pulled the stick right back and went up vertically under the belly of one of the 109's and pressed the button. I saw bullets tear into him for only a second. In my excitement I had thought nothing of the fact that I had lost air speed. In climbing I had been in almost a stalled position before the combat; my plane seemed to hang like a dead duck and then flicked over into a spin. Apparently I was not the only one who had done this. When I recovered from the spin I saw neither Hun nor Spitfire. The sky seemed empty but I had the feeling that a Hun might be waiting for me somewhere, so I kept a sharp lookout until I reached my base. Some were already back and others were coming in. We had smashed up the raid as well as some of the 109's and were now eagerly awaiting to be rearmed and refilled for the next patrol.

Although we did two more patrols that day we had no more luck. After that day's work we were ready for a good bath and a big dinner. We were as hungry as wolves and in good spirits.

Peter and I liked our new squadron and were looking forward to active service and happy days.

About a week later Peter was shot down with two others; those were the first losses since we had been with the squadron. Fortunately all three pilots were safe, having baled-out.

We had been ordered to take off during the lunch period – this frequently happened. We did not mind for we knew the call was urgent and even a few minutes could mean much.

Soon we were above the clouds at thirty-three thousand feet, leaving long white trails behind us, and climbing into the sun as much as possible. Although I admit excitement, I never again had the same feelings as on my first encounter. After stooging around for quite a while we were given a vector which brought us within sight of the enemies' smoke trails. In the distance they looked like little tadpoles. They were about the same height as us and they were still climbing to get the advantage, but in this they did not achieve their object. In a matter of seconds we sailed into them. Their only hope of escape was to dive vertically. This they did, but we were hot in pursuit and each man selected a victim. It is indeed good to get a Hun by oneself, but it is very hard to shoot straight doing 500 miles per hour.

My prey was not making much headway and he knew that he would have to make a fight for it, which turned out to be very uninteresting. He pulled out of a dive. I tried to get him as he was doing this, but failed to allow enough deflection. By this time he was going up vertically and rolling off the top when I was getting closer. I had the greater speed and he was almost stalled as he rolled over. I pressed the button whilst I was still upside down; it was a grand shot. Hot lead filled his engine and cockpit and pieces flew off the wings and fuselage. Yellow flames licked round the oil-soaked fuselage and he went down leaving a trail of black smoke.

Any momentary sympathy for my victim was quenched immediately by the memory of the women and children of London. In any case it was a fair fight and his chances were as good as mine.

When I arrived at the base I found that others had had the same good fortune but three of our men were missing and one was Peter. After two hours and still no sign of return I was much concerned and feared the worst.

We were relieved when the phone rang at the Dispersal Point and the Intelligence Officer announced that he had baled-out and landed in a tree but was unhurt.

With the knowledge of his safety my anxiety gave way to roars of laughter. We often wondered who would be first to be shot down and I thought it was just too funny. However, I had to return to the base the following day and enter by the back entrance, and it was Peter's turn to laugh. I had suffered a severe blow to my pride.

The following morning we were ordered off in the middle of our lunch. Needless to say, we had no tender thoughts towards the German Luftwaffe. As we gained height we learned over the R/T of the approach of a large raid coming towards the South-East coast. They were still some distance away, leaving us time to gain an altitude of thirty-four thousand feet, thus obtaining an advantageous position for attack.

The clouds were at a height of about 11,000 feet and of about eight-tenths density so that aircraft above were not visible from the ground. However, the Observer Corps had accurate information, and the controller gave us a vector which brought us within sight of the enemy aircraft, which seemed to stretch across the skies, at least 10,000 feet below us, like a swarm of locusts. We had the advantage of height, sun and speed, and with shouts of "Tally ho" and various other things we went screaming after them, each man for his own selection.

When the Boche saw us closing in for combat they all turned for their dear Fatherland, diving for protection in the clouds just before we got into range. It seemed like a game of hide-and-seek. There were 109's and Spitfires coming into view for the fraction of a second. It was hard not to give your colleagues a squirt.

After milling in and out of the clouds for about five minutes, I got the surprise and shock of my life. Some fortunate Hun had come out of the cloud right on my tail. My lovely Spitfire was riddled with machine-gun bullets and cannon shell. At the moment the bullets struck my machine, I felt as if some giant had hit me with a large hammer. (Often I had wondered if I should feel scared if I was unfortunate enough to be shot down; I learned through this bitter experience that one has not a second of time to spare for fear.) The impact was so great that it seemed to throw the machine forward. I felt a terrific smack in the back, and the stick jerked right out of my hand. At the same moment black fumes and smell of cordite filled the cockpit. Owing to holes in the bottom of the cockpit all manner of dust had blown up into my face and eyes.

I was tearing earthwards in a terrific wurzle. I was almost overcome by fumes, but after groping about I managed to find the oxygen regulator and to turn it full on. This blew the fumes away from my face and gave me a new strength and determination.

Although my eyes were streaming with water, I was able to see the fields getting larger, and for a moment visualized myself mixed up with the instrument panel and engine six feet below. After several attempts at baling-out had failed owing to the terrific pressure, and the fact that bullets had bent the runners of the hood, I managed, to my great relief, in gaining control of the machine. The air seemed to clear and after several attempts to start my engine had failed, I turned the ignition switches off and pulled up the petrol cocks, and, after tightening the Sutton harness, I prepared for a crash.

Far below I could see what appeared a possible landing-ground. Having decided to stick by my selection, I wiped the cold perspiration from my brow and surveyed the damage to the wings and cockpit. It was then that I was conscious of a stinging sensation on the edge of my leg – a bullet had passed through my boot, only scorching the flesh. In a few seconds I was approaching the ground when I noticed the field was pegged out with large stakes to make it impossible as a landing-ground for Germans. There was no turning back. I had to make the best of it. The poles were getting closer; one passed within a few inches of my port wing tip and just ahead more loomed up. I side-slipped away for I had considerable speed, with no flaps and wheels up. At that moment I hit the ground with a resounding crash; I thought that my ribs and neck had been broken. I careered along the ground for about 150 yards and went over on my back, and then all was quiet, except for the trickling of oil and petrol down the instrument panel. Men in battle-dress were soon on the scene and extricated me from the wreckage.

After a while I rested on an old farm roller and surveyed with sadness the ruins of my beautiful Spitfire.

"Have a cigarette," said someone sympathetically.

"No, thanks, I never smoke," and that look of compassion deepened.

I was treated as a hero, but I did not feel like one. "Care for a drink?" asked Mr. ——

"That's very kind of you," I said without a moment's hesitation, whereupon he took me by car to his house, and I tasted some of the best brandy I had had in years, together with an equally good blend of Scotch whisky. Mrs. —— must have thought I looked hungry for she had prepared an enormous meal of bacon, eggs and chips, which I did justice to in true R.A.F. style.

After attending to all the necessary arrangements, such as information as to where I was, what had happened, if I was all right, etc., Mr. —— took me back to the wreckage, where I made an examination to see if there was anything worth salvaging.

It was late in the afternoon. My hostess had a very good tea waiting for us when we got back to the house. I shall ever remember the kindness of these people.

I returned to my base the next day and was given a few days' leave, which was a great tonic. I felt like a million and was simply itching to see a Hun in my sights again and watch him spinning down in flames.

When war was in its junior stages I remember a certain general saying that the only good Hun was a dead one. I did not agree with that statement then but I am now fully convinced he was right.

My leave was over, and I left behind my people and

girl to return to the search for Huns.

The first patrol took place in the morning and we didn't have to explore long for a Hun. I think this one must have made a mistake. It was an ME. 110 and he was at a height of about 20,000 feet over the Thames Estuary, and had not seen our squadron approaching. What took place then was a sight for sore eyes. Almost every one had a pop at him: the wings and tail were shot clean off, and the fuselage hurtled earthwards in a ball of flame. That particular Hun must have found the heat very uncomfortable for we did not see him bale-out, or perhaps being born in a hell of a country he wouldn't notice the present hell. However, if it was too hot the Thames Estuary soon cooled him off.

It was towards the end of November that I took part in the most diverting combat in my life.

We were doing the usual Maidstone patrol in the morning when we saw some planes ahead diving for the clouds. According to information from ops., there was very little about, but we thought it wise to investigate. Soon we were screaming down after them at 450 m.p.h. through the clouds. Ahead we could see the planes, which to every one's disappointment were Hurricanes. Almost at the same instant a Spitfire could be seen going down vertically and straight into the deck, followed by a terrific explosion. He must have hit the deck at an approximate speed of 500 m.p.h. We came to the conclusion that he had blacked-out pulling out of the dive and couldn't have regained consciousness. To see such things as this shakes one considerably, but after re-forming above the clouds we had information of a Dornier molesting shipping some miles out at sea.

This took our minds right off the tragedy that had just occurred, and we were given a vector. The enemy's height was about 4,000 feet, so we went down to sea-level in order that he should not see us approaching.

After five minutes' flying the C.O. shouted, "Tally ho!" over the R/T and started to climb like hell. This was too good to be true: not more than 1,000 yards ahead the Dornier was toddling home unaware of the bloodthirsty squadron behind him.

The C.O. delivered his attack from close range followed quickly by two more Spitfires. I was about to go in when he made a steep turn to the right, I followed him round, firing all the time ahead of him. The return fire was yards away from me. Suddenly he dived almost vertically down to the sea, one of his engines leaving a trail of black smoke. Spitfires were diving at him from every direction, and the C.O. just above was refereeing and imploring us not to shoot each other.

The Hun was obviously finished after the first attack but every one wanted a pop at him. The language that followed was terrific. Charlie's section were shouting to others, "Get out of the way, I am about to come in firing," and Spitfires were doing head-on and quarter attacks all at the same time. How we avoided collision is a miracle.

The Hun must have thought it was a nightmare. The plane lasted only a few seconds, for he was in the drink and sank immediately. What fun we had crowded into a few seconds; there was only one of us with a few bullets in his plane. Some other Spitfire had fired a little too close, but very little damage was done and there was no ill feeling over it.

THE BATTLE OF BRITAIN
Blue section takes off, Dizzy leading.

INSTRUMENT PANEL OF A SPITFIRE

(*Top, l. to r.*): Durex, Rastus, Dizzy, Pookie.

SOME OF THE BOYS

(*Bottom, l. to r.*): Peter, Cookie, Billie, John, Dizzy, Duggie, Bogle, Johnnie, Ken, Lucky Leigh, Hugh, Apple.

"SCRAMBLE BASE."

Return of a Hero

(*L. to r.*): O'Reilly, Bogle, Christie, Lucky Leigh, Watty, Bob, Dizzy.

Crown copyright

THE "GREASE MONKEYS" TAKE OVER

DIZZY LOOKING MORBID

After the Battle

Wing-Commander A. S. Forbes, D.F.C.

(After the portrait by Eric Kennington).

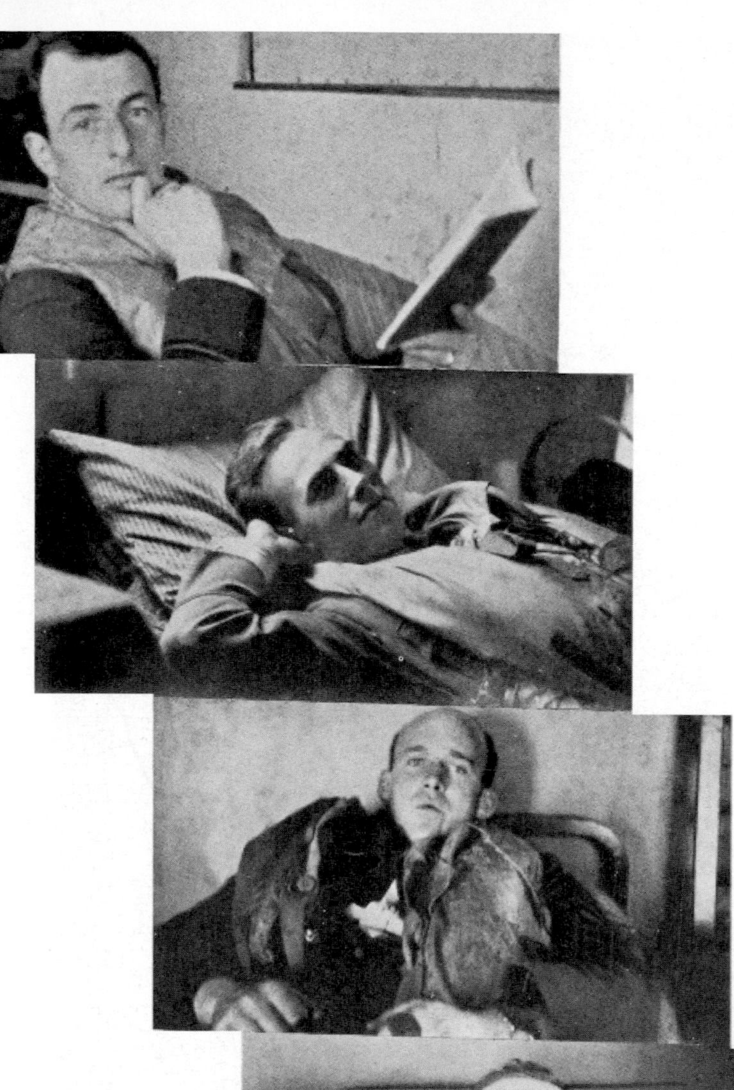

(*Top to bottom*):
Athol, Peter,
Bob Taylor,
Moonshine.

PICKLE ABOUT TO DO A CHANNEL SHOW

End of a Hun

I had some doubt as to which was the more dangerous, attacking one Hun with ten Spitfires, or ten Huns with one Spitfire.

Christmas was approaching and fewer Huns were molesting us during the day, so our squadron was ordered to return to our home base in Scotland. It was indeed a well-earned rest, and I welcomed the chance of seeing the splendour of the Scottish mountains and lochs from a plane. One can see so much at once from a great height. Where else in the world could one find scenery to surpass that in Scotland?

It seemed so unnatural to fly without a Hun in the vicinity, or to fly without having to worry about your tail.

We were there only five days when the squadron was split up; some went to O.T.U. as instructors, and one or two out East, whilst Peter and I were appointed to a new squadron.

It was with some regret that we left our old squadron, for they were a splendid set of fellows and we had enjoyed many happy times together.

However, twenty-four hours after leaving Scotland we were meeting our new colleagues. The Squadron-Leader D.F.C., V.M., Oxo, Dizzie, Bogle, The Duke, Butch, Pickle, Moldy and Durex, the latter being known to Peter and me at F.T.S.

We received such welcome as amply compensated for our former regrets, on land and in the air their companionship has been in keeping with that welcome, and it is with confidence that Peter and I look forward to many more combats with the truest and bravest of men.

Editor's Note

Before finishing all that he intended to write, poor old Max was posted "missing" after a Channel dogfight. A grand fellow, how we missed him!

INTRODUCING DIZZY

Dizzy is rather an unusual type – shortish, stocky, red-headed, freckle-faced, and looks kind of tough and wild. When first I took the squadron over his behaviour was, as the name implied, very dizzy – fun and games, schoolboy pranks and all the rest of it, wrapped into one. His general appearance would be classed as "scruffy," especially when seen in flying kit. His tunic is one of the oldest to be found and his hair is never, with the exception of a few moments before parties, anything but unruly – somehow it sticks up and outward. Amongst his flying kit one of his proudest possessions is the seventh veil of a seven-veil dancer. I won't go into details as to how he acquired it, but it was all in fair play. Dizzy has a few peculiarities: for instance his laugh is really peculiar and sounds like nothing you have ever heard before. When he is really pleased with something his pet expression is "Charming, charming."

When I arrived he was the senior Flying Officer; when his Flight-Commander was posted and he took over the flight, overnight he went through one of those peculiar changes which sometimes occur. He became pretty serious-minded, and kept his schoolboy pranks and what not to out of working hours and tackled the job of being Flight-Commander magnificently.

There is so much difference between Bob and Dizzy that it is not possible to compare them as Flight-Commanders, for in their particular way they each excelled. I could not possibly have had better right-hand men.

Dizzy's Story

VIVIDLY do I remember my first encounter with the Hun. I had been in the squadron about a month and was extremely fortunate to gain valuable operational knowledge after such a short while. The encounter took place some eighty miles out to sea (I still shudder at the thought) and I attacked as No. 3 of my section. It was a Junkers 88 and I recall how, instead of concentrating on the enemy as I thought I would do, I was more concerned with my instruments – that was until I got within range, of course. I had expected that I would be alarmed by the fire of the rear gunner, but to my surprise I was totally unmoved by it. As soon as I was within range I let him have it, aiming at the aeroplane in general instead of concentrating on the engines, as I would do now. I killed the rear gunner and when I left him – the other two of the section finished before I did – he was pouring glycol from one engine. It struck me on the run home that not once had I noticed a swastika or even absorbed details of the aircraft. The thing had somehow seemed ominous and un-British. Recognition had not been necessary. Straining my eyes for that welcome glimpse of land, and checking my compass with the sun, I returned to England, home and beauty, feeling quite a dog and a goer despite the fact that my score was but one-third of a damaged JU. 88. The experience gained, however, proved extremely useful in the future.

After this encounter, there was a lull of a few months,

during which we spent our flying time in practice dogfights – both a spectacular and useful pastime – mock attacks and interceptions, displays for various notabilities and the inevitable girl friend, and innumerable unsuccessful interception patrols. On one occasion I was having a dogfight with Billy. I was both inexperienced and not too fit at the time and one of my evasive tactics was a roll off the top of a loop. I hung on top for a bit and the petrol in the exhaust manifolds burned solidly for about ten seconds – it seemed like ten hours. I thought that Billy had given me a squirt and that I was on fire. On landing my face was the colour of green cheese and Billy (then my Flight-Commander) made me accompany him on a four-mile run that evening in order to get me in trim. Dear old Billy!

Another of our more serious tasks was to do convoy patrols and many an hour did I spend floating backwards and forwards over convoys, wondering what it was like to be sailing the seas with aircraft droning overhead. What I was particularly interested in was to discover what the sailors thought of us airmen. Whether they thought we were a set of over-publicised young scatterbrains or whether they bore the same admiration for us as we do for them – they the men who strive against storm and tempest, submarine and enemy bombs.

Gradually the war in the air began to develop. Things down south got hotter. More and more enemy aircraft were shot down. We began to "flap" more often. Monthly flying hours increased. The boys began to shoot down and chase more Huns. We shot down six on six successive days. Then came my second encounter with the enemy. A Dornier 215 was spotted at 27,000 feet by Pickles, who was No. 3 in the section. Sergeant "S" was leader and I was No. 2. We gave chase and caught him about forty miles out to sea at 10,000 feet. Sergeant "S" closed to attack and I came up abreast of him to distract the rear gunners. We fired simultaneously, broke, and attacked again. He was obviously hit. Pickles attacked and I watched him. He came up like a bat out of hell and broke sharply, nearly colliding with the stricken Hun, smoke pouring from his eight Brownings. Return fire stopped, we went in again and Jerry turned round for England – the sign of surrender. We followed closely, watching for any signs of a trap. Smoke poured from his engines, he was in a bad way. Suddenly his nose dropped and he dived almost vertically. A most impressive sight it was, the huge twin-engined machine hurtling earthwards with great streams of smoke following it. Down, down, down – would he never pull out? I wondered. He didn't. With the most terrific splash I'd ever seen he hit the sea and disintegrated. I circled the spot but could see nothing but oil. I was jubilant; my second engagement and successful. Life was very full. I flew back at zero feet and cut some capers over a lightship on the way.

A few days after this we had some momentous news. We were ordered to go down south where the big air blitz of 1940 was just beginning. Within twelve hours we had packed our bags and moved off. I remember wondering as we flew over our old base in a squadron beat-up, how many of these lads would be alive to tell the tale in a couple of months.

On landing at our new base we were ordered off almost immediately on patrol, from which we all returned without seeing anything. I landed feeling rather disgruntled and thinking that all the tales of mass attacks were so much rot. I was soon to be disillusioned.

Next morning we went off at dawn to an advance base and after a hasty breakfast we were ordered to scramble. Off we went. I felt a little frightened. At 20,000 feet over Dover we suddenly sighted about 100 aircraft coming from the direction of London. "Aha!" I thought. "Here it comes."

The squadron headed for the formations, which were being attacked by other of our fighters. We burst into the middle of the fighters and bombers and I singled out a formation of four Heinkels below me.

Down I went at about 450 m.p.h., and pulling up I squirted the bomber on the port side of the formation. Black smoke oozed from his port engine. I came down again, squirted the whole formation and after observing four or five ME. 109's in my mirror I thought, "Plenty of time, pal, fifty per cent of people are bumped off in their first big scrap." So down went the old nose and at about 500 m.p.h. I screeched earthwards.

The Intelligence Officer was waiting for me as I landed and I told him I had damaged a Heinkel. Then he passed on to the next man. Every one was bubbling over with excitement. Each man had fired at something and several were able to claim certainties. Two of the boys had baled-out and had thus become members of the famous Caterpillar Club. It was a successful beginning to our sojourn down south, for we had bagged five certainties and three probables and others damaged.

From then on life became a series of hastily eaten meals

which were often missed altogether; patrols at all hours of the day and binges in the evenings when we were not so dog-tired that we had to go to bed.

On my second patrol I had a narrow escape which warned me of the danger of being caught napping. We had engaged a large number of German fighters and all I could see was a large number of aircraft milling round in every conceivable attitude. Suddenly I saw an ME. 109 just below me and in my ignorance went straight at him, shooting as I went. The next thing I knew was that something hit me from behind, that my guns had stopped firing and that I was spinning down. One glance in my mirror showed me two or three ME. 109's coming after me. I came out of the spin and continued in a vertical attitude at something over 500 m.p.h. I pulled out at 5,000 feet and then found that one of my ailerons did not work and that all my electrical gear was unserviceable. Hurriedly pinpointing my position, I headed for base, keeping a wary eye open for forced landing-fields as I did so. On reaching my base I approached to land and while holding off, my wing suddenly dropped. I thought that I was going to pile up, but fortunately I kept her going. It was due to the disturbance of the aileron balance. As I taxied in I saw another aeroplane land with one aileron completely shot off by a cannon shell.

On examination I found that two of my aileron wires were completely shot away, my radio set was punctured and there were seven bullet holes directly behind my armour plate. Phew!

The next day we went up as usual and mixed it with large numbers of ME. 109's. I had not been able to get a bead on anything and was manœuvring for position when I saw an aircraft getting into position behind me. I adopted violent evasive action and came out just behind it, when I saw that it was a Spitfire which then sheared off. Whether or not the pilot would have taken a short squirt at me I do not know, for one fighter looks very much like another from astern and in a mêlée. I did not have any success that day, but when on my way back to my base at 1,000 odd feet, I saw an aeroplane falling at a colossal speed from the sky. When at about 500 feet it flicked on to its back and hit the earth at something like 600 m.p.h. There was a violent explosion and a sheet of flame was all that remained. High above I saw a parachute floating idly down. Lucky for him he was not in that plane!

The next patrol brought more fortune in its train, for we saw a huge HE. 111 separated from its squadron attempting an unobtrusive getaway to Germany. Two of us left the squadron to deal with this intruder and after a few squirts I could see the huge propellers ticking over. He then made a crash-landing in a wood clearing, and the other bloke and I saw three of the crew get out – the fourth just wasn't, I expect. While they clustered round the wreck we circled the spot until some "brown jobs" took them prisoner. As soon as they were in safe hands I dived straight at them and did an "upward Charlie" over them – not good for the engine but I thought it excusable! The fact that only three men got out set me pondering on the subject of air gunners. The pluck of a man who can stay at his post with such machines as Spitfires and Hurricanes, or for that matter even ME. 109's, attacking him is inconceivable. Horrid tales are often told about rear gunners being scraped into jampots and the like. For my part I have nothing but admiration for them.

Despite its hardships, however, the few weeks during which the blitz was in full swing will rank as some of the happiest of my life. The spirit of the squadron and the moral uplift of such personality as our then C.O. was incredible. Life was cheap and the general atmosphere was devil-may-care, but some of the scenes in our combined mess and pilots' room were indescribable. How can one do justice on paper to such scenes as when Happy, intelligence officer, fell downstairs clad only in a bath towel and a tin hat when the siren went for immediate danger; or how Pickles pinched the kitty of our poker school when we were ordered off one day, and went chasing out to his aeroplane yelling that he was going to get shot down so that we would lose our money?

Shortly afterwards we were ordered to move to a new base and, amid much cursing, the stores and transport left by road. The squadron flew to our new base, which we found immensely to our liking, as there was a noticeable lack of formality around the place. After the scramble for rooms had subsided, we celebrated that night by having a colossal binge. After taking down Happy's trousers and washing his abdomen with beer, we decided to go to bed, well pleased with our day's work.

Dawn broke next day to find us at readiness with a special mission to perform. Oxo, Camy and yours truly had to protect a machine which was spotting for our shore batteries. Off we went and patrolled Calais while all the flak in Germany appeared to open upon us. We were there for an hour before the spotter turned for home, and like so many sheep-dogs guarding their flock we took it home. A very interesting experience it was too.

The next few days passed peacefully enough, the only incidents of note being when we found several bombers limping home over the coast. We finished them off without any opposition. It proved to be, however, just the calm before the storm.

September 15th, 1940, dawned clear and bright. We arose with the dawn, and everything appeared as it always did. We were ordered up on patrol just as I was playing chess with Happy. "Hang on, Happy," I yelled, "be with you in an hour or two!" and off we went. No sooner had we got to our height than we saw a formation of bombers and fighters just above us. "O.K., boys," the C.O. called, "we're going up to 'em," and getting right under the formation we all climbed right into the middle. I was number 2 to the C.O. – I always was – and followed him right up. I was just about stalled when we were in the middle so I levelled out, and let 'em pass me, shooting as I did. You could almost see the look of surprise on the faces of those Dorniers. At one moment they were sailing along *en route* for London, and the next minute twelve Spitfires simply grew among them. They broke up in every conceivable angle and attitude. At one moment there was a close formation of bombers; at the next there were thirty odd hapless Dorniers all over the sky with no chance in the world.

After making my head-on attack and giving the pilot of one bomber apoplexy by refusing to break until I could smell the garlic in his breath, I turned at about "12 G" (or thereabouts) and came round on his tail. After a squirt or two, one of his engines blew up, sending oil and glycol all over my windscreen, and the other was beginning to burn. I waved good-bye and looked for more. I saw a HE. 111 making for cloud below me, so screaming down I opened fire at extreme range and broke at the last possible moment. I thought I'd hit him because my controls were so stiff at the speed I was travelling that I only just scraped by. I climbed above him and watched. His whole tail unit was on fire and his engines were smoking. I came down for another squirt just before he went into cloud, and whilst I was squirting he vanished from sight and was seen no more (I hope). On landing, I found that we had got rid of twelve for certain with many more probables. But I was extremely annoyed because that twerp Happy only gave me one certain of my two.

My feelings were partly alleviated to find that the Royal Air Force had accounted for 185 Jerry planes that day. Maybe my certainty-which-was-only-a-probable was not so important after all.

The next few days were quieter, but soon we had another good day. We suddenly intercepted some ME. 109's over the coast and I protected Oxo's tail, while he got busy on one. It blew up after two short squirts, then we got together and went after four more. "It's O.K., pal," I called to Oxo, "they're friendly, I think." "Mebbe you're right," he replied, "but we'll just make sure." Then, "Christ, they're 109's!" Up we went. I took on two, Oxo took on the other two. I squirted one and he went for home. Fastening on to the tail of the other I gave him a good one. His nose went down vertically. I followed. Down we screeched at 400. We passed the coast, I squirted again, keeping a wary eye open for his boy friend. Suddenly his speed dropped and I saw a stream of glycol. "You poor blighter," I thought. Then I gave him a long one. Pieces fell off. He faltered, then hit the sea and vanished. I looked around but saw nothing, and so returned at zero feet feeling a prize shocker.

The next engagement we had was against the much-vaunted Messerschmitt 110. We saw them being chased by some Hurricanes. Being decent types, we nipped in to help. I'd never seen a 110 before, and seeing twin-engined machines, I thought for a moment that they were bombers, and consequently made a head-on attack at them. I soon realised my folly, and delivered a normal attack, after having shot through the whole formation head-on. I was doing nearly 400 m.p.h., and they were nigh on 300 m.p.h., and we were passing each other at about 700 m.p.h., which is pretty fast. I fired all the time, but could not observe the effect. By the time I had turned to follow them they were miles away. I followed hard, but could only catch up with a straggler, who was being fired at by a couple of Hurricanes. It was their meat, so I left them to it. I particularly noticed that the 110's would go straight for a short while, and then form a defensive circle, thus making a somewhat erratic progress home. I learned later that of the twenty or more that came over, about fifteen were shot down.

As I was returning to my base, I saw a Hurricane ahead of me, and decided to test his awakedness. I made a mock attack on him, but before I got into range he had whirled round in a tight Immelmann. I flew alongside and stuck up a couple of fingers, to which he grinningly replied. He certainly had all his wits about him.

At dawn next day operations asked for a pilot to make a weather reconnaissance of the Channel, so off I went. I snooped around about mid-Channel but the fish weren't biting, so I had to return somewhat despondent.

We were sent off next day as per usual – Jerry had not yet got fed up with us – and whilst patrolling I saw a 109 in the distance. I was rather behind the squadron, having been delayed on the take-off by a rigger – not my usual one – who had forgotten to switch on my main oxygen supply, so I didn't bother to tell any one, but slipped off unobserved. I appeared to catch him napping because I got right under him before I fired. Then I gave him three seconds of hot lead right in the guts. He shook a bit, turned to see what it was, then continued on his way. I noticed the tell-tale stream of glycol, but closed for another bang. Full and square I hit him, and saw his tail struts fall off, and a large piece of fuselage, probably his hood, was jettisoned. He went down just on top of a cloud layer, and carried on. Swearing under my breath, I caught him up, got right up to him and gave him the full works. Black smoke oozed, and he fell through the cloud. I followed, and found myself north of Dungeness. But could I see that benighted Jerry? Could I hell? I circled the spot for a quarter of an hour, looking, looking, looking. I was then at 4,000 feet, and a 109 with most of its guts shot away could only at the best reach the sea at that height. I had to return in a flaming temper, and told Happy where to look. He found nothing and so I was only given a probable. Probable my foot. If that Jerry so much as got half-way across the Channel I'd eat my longerons.

That night we had an all-squadron binge in the nearby

town. Pickles had three half-pints of bitter, and changed from a nervous, quiet schoolboy into a lusty, noisy, excitable young man. It is no exaggeration to say that he has never been the same man since – an amazing phenomenon. We arrived back in the small hours, threw furniture at each other and then went to bed.

There was a bit of a lull after this. Jerry had changed his tactics from large numbers of bombers and small fighter escorts, and then few bombers and many fighters, and was now on the all-fighter stage where their value was merely nuisance. They always flew very high, and would come in and drop a few bombs and then go back again. This didn't give a lot of time for interception purposes, but we often had a crack at them.

We were chasing some who were a bit higher than we were one day, and we all got split up. I was after one bloke at over 32,000 feet over the Channel, and was slowly gaining on him. By the time I got within range we were over France, and so I lost no time, but gave one short burst and then a very long one from about 400 yards. I had obviously hit him, and he turned over and went down vertically in a cloud of white smoke. He may have landed safely, or he may have gone straight into the deck, so I could only claim a damaged for that. I returned towards England, when suddenly my windscreen was covered with oil. Hastily checking my instruments, I saw my oil pressure registering zero and the glycol and oil temperatures rising. I switched off the engine and prepared to force-land. I had plenty of height, but a long way to go, so I headed for the nearest part of the coast. I crossed at about 3,000 feet, and just made an aerodrome. I had no height in which to turn into wind, and so I had to land down-wind. I came over the boundary fast – always better to over-shoot than under-shoot – and held off. She floated for hundreds of yards with the wind, and when she touched down it was obvious that I was going into the boundary hedge. I had my brakes full on, but the grass was wet.

Just as the hedge loomed up, I put my hand on my gunsight to protect my head. That was the last thing I remembered for a little while, and when I came to my first instinct was to get out of the aeroplane. I had no idea where I was, or how I came to be there. A night in bed was enough, and I returned to my station next day by road, and went home for a few days' sick leave.

When I got back after my sick leave, I found that the weather had been too bad for much flying, so I didn't miss much. After I had once again settled down we had another considerable "do" with the Nazi fighters. I had a hangover from a cold at the time and was not really fighting fit. The 109's had formed a defensive circle at about 30,000 feet, and we were endeavouring to break it up.

Eventually they split up all over the sky, and I lost sight of them. I was tooling around at about 15,000 feet, the height to which I imagined they had gone, and, incidentally, was keeping a wary eye in at least three dimensions, when I suddenly heard a rattle behind me. I swung instinctively, and a 109 with a huge red nose flashed past me, levelled out, and then did a complete flick roll before going earthwards. I was so surprised that I didn't get a bead on him. I followed him down, vowing vengeance, and at about 2,000 feet we crossed over Dungeness.

Then a 109, followed by a Spitfire, flashed across my

bows, in a manner of speaking, and momentarily distracted my attention. Then I looked again, the original 109 had disappeared. I looked everywhere, but could not find him. To this day I feel sure he went straight into the sea, but as I didn't see him I could claim nothing. I swore in three different languages, and climbed to look for more trouble. I found it in the shape of another Hun coming towards me. I gave him a quickee head-on and then he had gone. I turned and saw another Spitfire come down on him, smoke pouring from his guns. "Aha," methought, "your number's up!" and then, still looking round, I returned home.

Then came the lull. Nothing happened for weeks. The newspapers began to gloat over our victories and we got fed-up because we couldn't repeat them. Reaction set in, and we went haywire. I remember one night when we came home in a convoy of three cars, with toilet paper streaming from them. Every car we passed would get some toilet paper, and many were the verbal exchanges we had. One night we had a terrific "beat-up" in the mess. Busts were blackleaded to look like Hitler, much cock-fighting and wrestling took plate. We blacked Pickles' face to look like a nigger boy, dressed up in the most alarming attire, and finished the night by being hounded up and down corridors and around the house and grounds by a Pickles gone completely balmy.

Soon after this we moved to a new base where we settled down to station routine, after a long spell of single-squadron bases. We had been there about a fortnight when we had seen no action and were pretty well browned off. Then came that glorious day.

We intercepted about 40 JU. 87's accompanied by some

escorting fighters, just before they reached their target, a coastal town. I was one of a section dispatched to intercept a single raider when we spotted them.

I rubbed my eyes when I saw these lumbering dive-bombers; I couldn't believe that it could be true. Then, with a howl of delight, I went straight into the middle. The next few minutes were spent by me in attacking and breaking up innumerable formations of these. I saw two break sharply and jettison their bombs, obviously hit. Then I made a longer attack on another who heeled over with oil pouring from his engine. I had not time to follow him down as I was too busy attacking the others. My technique was to go straight for the sections from every conceivable angle until they split up their formation. It was an impressive sight as we battled over the target. I could see the 87's go down vertically on to the target, and drop their bombs to the accompaniment of ack-ack of every calibre. Huge columns of water rose as the bombs exploded, and flashes and shell-bursts could be seen everywhere. In the general mêlée I saw Spitfires attacking from everywhere, with their guns smoking as they fired. One man fired as he was on his back – or maybe I was on my back – I couldn't tell.

Aircraft disintegrated around me. I saw them catch fire, go straight down, smoking, into the sea. It was vivid. Dante would have gone into ecstasies if he could have changed places with me. Satan would have found the atmosphere quite homelike. It was the acme of aerial combat. Flame, smoke, gunpowder, death, and hell, all mixed up; undoubtedly the finest moment of my life.

The formations had been split up. Individual dive-bombers were left awaiting attack. "Enough," I thought.

"Now for the kill." The next "87" I saw dive down, I followed. I saw his bomb drop harmlessly into the sea, and then came the attack. Tracer bullets, cannon shells, explosive shells, every type of ground defence was in action. They were firing at my chosen target, but I was close behind, and got the benefit of quite a lot. My "87" was at last out of range of ground defences, and I could at last get down to business. I wiped the ice off my windscreen, and made a quarter attack on him. I closed right up to him before he broke, but there was no fire from the rear gunner. I realised by this time that my ammunition must be getting short, and that I had better finish him off before it ran out. I closed to point-blank range, accordingly, and fired deliberately, taking careful aim. I saw my explosive ammunition hit its mark. A thin tongue of flame crept from the port side of his engine. I climbed above him and watched the flame gradually spread; it welled up until it surrounded the cockpit. The nose of the "87" gradually fell, and then he went right into the sea. He hit the water with a huge splash, and vanished. Only oil was left. I circled the spot, saw nothing and then returned home, observing a few holes in my wings as I went. When I landed I found that one of my ailerons was held by only two strands of wire, and, incidentally, that at least seventeen of the raiders had perished.

The next incident of any note that occurred was when we went up on an interception patrol in rather bad weather. We did not see any Jerries, and on our return found that the weather had deteriorated very badly, and that there was thick fog over Southern England. We were trying to find our base, and time was passing, till eventually

I was flying with my eyes on my petrol gauge nearly the whole time. By the grace of God we just made an aerodrome and as I landed I heard voices on the radio. As each pilot landed he expressed his relief by blasphemy, foul cursing, and any other thing that came into his strained brain. It was rather amusing to listen to as one sat on good old Mother Earth, but it might have proven a disastrous trip. We had a terrific party that night, and slept on the floor of a friend's house.

A few days later we took off on another patrol, and just as we had gained our necessary height my aircraft suddenly jerked violently, and the nose of another aeroplane suddenly appeared vertically in front of me. My airscrew was knocked off and my lateral controls were non-effective. I opened up my hood, most of which was knocked off anyway, parts missing my head by inches, and contemplated the situation (in a manner of speaking).

My aircraft was obviously seriously damaged: I might possibly make a forced landing but it was dubious, as there was a ground mist, and I would not be able to see hills, trees, and things until I had hit them. Further, my much weakened airframe might be in the process of disintegration for all I knew. Accordingly, I loosened my straps, looked at the altimeter, which showed 5,000 feet, and let the airflow pull me out of the cockpit with my hand on the rip-cord.

Next thing I knew was that I was floating earthwards with a huge silk canopy over my head. I gasped with relief, for my decision had of necessity been hurried and I had not considered the possibility of my parachute not opening.

On reaching the ground I hung up a thirty-foot tree for

some time in the middle of a wood, whilst I could hear the Army, Home Guard, and sundry others crashing through the undergrowth towards me. I detached myself from the parachute and swarmed down the tree. On reaching the ground I was greeted by two small boys who had magically appeared before the authorities had. One of them said to me, "How are you, mister?" to which I managed to reply politely, "Fine, thank you." Then came the Army, rifles in hand, followed by the Home Guard, and finally an old farmer, shot-gun in hand, his devout spouse clinging to his trousers, apparently trying to hold him back. I took a quick swig of brandy from my flask, and then felt equal, at the worst, to a charge of buckshot in my nether regions.

I managed to shake off the authorities, and found a good type of Army officer with a couple of buxom wenches, who took me to their delightful home, and there ladled up the largest whisky and spot of soda I had ever seen. The police were kicking up a bit of a shindy outside, jealous, I expect, so I bid my charming hostesses adieu, and stopping only to sign their visitor's book, departed back to my squadron via the police station and an Army car.

I went up as usual next day, but for the first quarter of an hour felt distinctly uneasy. There followed a lull of a few days, and then a large stroke of luck when my section was ordered to intercept a single raider, whilst we were on patrol. Within five minutes of receiving the order I had spotted him. He saw me too, for he turned hot-foot for home. No use, however, for my Spitfire was faster than his 109. I caught him up, and after two very short bursts, he had caught fire and baled-out. I only used twenty rounds from each gun on him.

That ended for me the Blitz of 1940. The new year is well on its way now, and the weather has restricted all aerial warfare. We have, however, made our first big offensive against the enemy. This means that after a year of quite active service, the Royal Air Force Fighter Command has slowly but surely turned from defensive to offensive operations. Now the air is full of talk of invasion. Who cares? We've beaten 'em once, and we'll beat 'em again.

The victory of 1940 was not won without loss to ourselves, however, and there is many a happy memory to be had by looking back through old photographs of the squadron, wherein old familiar faces crop up. The memory of those brave lads who lost their lives in the defence of their country will never die. They had everything to live for and yet full of self-sacrifice, they laid down their lives for their country. It was done twenty years ago; it is being done to-day. And what of the future? Who knows?

INTRODUCING ATHOL

Athol, our beloved C.O., took over from equally beloved Lucky Leigh in October, 1940. The old boy of the squadron, being some thirty years of age, he is tallish, slim, and looks a bit of a Casanova. He has slanting, deep-set green eyes, a large beak-like nose, and rather long hair curling up over each ear and looking like a pair of horns, so that when he gets a certain gleam in his eye he looks exactly like Old Nick himself.

Without doubt Athol is one of the most pleasant blokes alive – I never knew him in a bad mood. Being of a most hospitable nature and always ready for a party, his wine bill was something phenomenal. Absolutely without fear, he is exceptional as a leader, having that happy knack of inspiring his pilots to great efforts; Binder Corbin always used to say that Athol's idea of an afternoon's sport was to fly around the gasometers in Berlin.

His somewhat lazy nature is offset by his outstanding ability for organising things, and especially for getting other people to work for him.

He has another characteristic in his ability to wipe the wing off any car sooner or later without seriously damaging it – especially after some of his parties.

Beloved by all his squadron, he is one of the best.

Athol's Story

ALREADY one could see it was going to be a magnificent day. There was enough light to see the outlines of those huge chunks of cumulus clouds, but there was some time to sunrise and the morning cold. A heavy dew had fallen during the night and as I plodded over to my machine, not much more than a silhouette on the skyline, the dew made my boots wet. I only hoped it wouldn't soak into the fleece lining.

The crew were there, busy wiping the machine down after the morning run up. S., the rigger, came forward and took my parachute and went to put it in the machine; R., the fitter, came round and told me she was in good trim. A grand pair to have as a crew – they kept that Spitfire spotless both inside and out; there just wasn't a thing wrong with her. The slightest hint, and they'd put in hours of extra work to track the fault down and if there wasn't any, they'd just say, "It's as well to make sure; it might develop." Strange to think that on these two and a few others one's very life depended. If they made mistakes or forgot to do something, then the machine might pack up during a combat, if not before.

After our usual natter, I climbed into the machine and checked over the instruments, controls and equipment, then signed up the machine's history sheet. Yes, they'd topped up with petrol after the morning run-up. Everything was set for the coming day.

I strolled back to the Dispersal Hut. Most of the others

were there, putting their "Mae West's" on and making last-minute adjustments to their varied flying clothing.

I was ready, so I flopped into the nearest chair. My feet and hands were cold, but there wasn't any heat coming from the fire, so I sat back so that I could see what was happening. For the best part every one was quiet – somehow, there's not much to say at 4.30 in the morning: it's later, just before breakfast, that people begin to tell of the previous night's adventures.

Every now and then, the cursed phone bell would ring and every one would look over at the instrument, hoping that they would catch the gist of the conversation. It was mostly "Ops." making a few inquiries or passing on some information. Up to date, it appeared that there was "nothing on board" of any interest. A few Huns out on reconnaissance had been reported, but they were well out to sea.

One or two of the blokes had dropped off into an uneasy doze; now and then there would be a few muttered words between the others; or someone would get up and look out of the window, maybe open the door and step outside.

Being somewhat older than the others – nearly thirty, whilst their average age is about twenty-two – I always look on these scenes with interest. Since we moved south into the blitz area, there have been quite a few changes in the half-dozen or so that came with us. The other – well, they're either gone or in hospital. Only one posted – his nerves wouldn't stand the racket.

I found it interesting to speculate as to what was going on in their minds; did they think and feel the same way about things as I did; were they standing the strain better or not as well as myself? There was no contradicting that it was tough going. We flew most of the daylight hours, had little time off and were obliged to snatch meals as and when we could. As for sleep, that was reduced to a point where one felt exhausted by mid-morning with more than the average man's day still ahead of us. But what of these not such good things? We had a big job to do and by God we'd see it through or go to hell, every man Jack.

Young Starkey was in bad shape this morning. I hoped we wouldn't have too bad a day for his sake. He badly needed a rest, but then there was no one to replace him for the moment.

Time dragged by, the sun was beginning to rise and with it little swirls of ground mist rose from odd hollows. David was busy writing a letter, most probably to that girl friend he'd told me about; Muzzy was happily sleeping, snoring like an old sow; Ginger was tying and untying knots in a piece of string; Butch was just looking straight ahead of him, thinking no doubt, but from his expression you couldn't tell.

Just at this moment the phone bell went again. As usual, every one became silent, motionless, with a slight strain to catch the words before they were spoken. Then, from the conversation and expression on the orderly's face, we knew we were off. There was a scraping of chairs, a few grunts, and then a general rush for the door. A yell from one of the pilots sent the crews racing to their machines, closely followed by the pilots.

Within a few moments of that shout, the first engine started with a roar, breaking the beautiful quiet of the summer's morning; within seconds, all twelve motors were running, there was a short lull as the pilots strapped themselves into their seats, then machine after machine started taxi-ing out to the runway.

The sun had risen fairly high by now and the morning mists had almost cleared. As we went, I saw the sparkle of the sun on the grass reflected by the dewdrops.

Somehow one can't help wondering in these last moments of earthliness with all the beauties of nature around, just how many are to see them again.

As I taxied out I always said a wee prayer – "Please God help us all."

With well-practised drill, the machines lined up on the end of the runway; with a wave from the leader, we started. Spit. after Spit. leapt forward at full throttle, up came their tails and away we climbed, circling the aerodrome for a short while until we had formed up, then we swung east, climbing for all we were worth.

All this time I had been working hard; taxi-ing takes up one's attention. Taking off and getting into your allotted position is more automatic and as I did so I looked at the two blokes on either side of me, Ginger to right and Butch to left. They were both busy doing things inside their machines, but suddenly Butch looked up. His oxygen mask and helmet hid most of his face. I knew he gave me one of those quick sheepish smiles of his, just as he sometimes did when we were back on the deck. Then we got on with the business in hand.

Up and up we circled, the broken cumulus were at about 12,000 feet; beautifully outlined by the blue sky above them, they flashed past as we climbed beyond. It was getting appreciably colder and I was feeling hungry – 15,000 feet. I turned my oxygen on and took deep breaths; I had been feeling the lack of it for the past couple of minutes.

I wondered what this trip would bring with it – not as bad as the last trip yesterday, I hoped.

I turned my oxygen on another 1,000 feet and looked round my instruments. We were climbing fast, but the oil and coolant temperatures were normal. I switched on my sight, turned the safety catch on the firing button and went through all the other checks automatically.

Ops. hadn't had much to say since we took off. Apparently there were a dozen or more Huns allegedly floating around somewhere near Dungeness. They were supposed to be at some twenty-five or thirty thousand feet, so on we went, climbing flat out. Up to thirty-two – then, in order to get the advantage of the sun, we swept off towards the east. Down below us, like a plasticine model, we could see the whole of the south-east of England, and on the other side of the Channel, France, but somehow not the France I'd been to so often, but a nasty, dark, gloomy France. This was only due to the cloud formation over land, but it did somehow seem symbolical. We crossed the coast and circled out to sea, coming in towards Dungeness, hoping to catch the Hun unawares. Everybody's eyes were straining, straining for those little black dots that meant – well, who knew what?

We were still travelling at full speed – the controller had just told us that the Hun had turned and was on his way out. If we met them it would most probably mean a head-on, and I must say I'm not keen on the idea of a head-on with the 109. I don't mind machine-guns, but I've a great deal of respect for that cannon – it pushes out a nasty big chunk and only the other day I saw what it could do when Starkey came back with three hits on his machine. Ginger is sitting apparently motionless, staring straight ahead of him. Butch caught my eye and gave me a wave – that wave expressed everything. I knew Butch well, he had been with us the whole time. We'd trained together and here we were for the "nth" time chasing the Hun. Still no sign of him – we were well over Dungeness by now, not quite but almost up sun; if we were ever going to meet him, now was the ideal time. I can quite imagine everybody's face, straining like hell to catch just a fleeting glimpse of those dots so that they could give the warning and everybody would train their eyes in the right direction. I was just telling myself that we had missed them – Ginger had put his thumb down when there was a yell of "Tally ho" on the R/T. I scanned the whole horizon in one quick flash – still I couldn't see them, but whilst I was wondering where they could be, the squadron wheeled left and then settled down on steady course. We were going flat out now, diving slightly towards France. I searched every square inch of the sky and I'm damned if I could see a thing.

On we went, streaking down at full throttle, and suddenly, just as I thought the leader was crazy, there they were! I'll never be quite certain whether there were twelve or fourteen – they were rather spread out. For once we were going to have the jump on them, that is, if we could catch them up, for they also were streaking ahead. They'd got a good start of us, but I don't think they knew we were so close to them. Very gradually, we were overtaking them. We still had plenty of height over them. With a very slight turn, the rate of the dive increased; we began losing height rapidly; we were getting closer and closer. For one split second I looked over the machine at the other two. They were in good position. We were all set and approaching rapidly for a perfect attack. Just as I thought we'd a sitting target with only about 500 yards to go, one of the brutes must have seen us for, like a flash, the formation broke up, diving in all directions. A quick command on the R/T and each of us picked his own particular Hun. Mine jammed his stick forward and went down in, as near as damn it, a vertical dive. We were at twenty-three thousand when we started. I lost sight of him under the nose but soon I got him in view again. Down and down we went; hell, but my eardrums were hurting. It was no good – he was travelling faster than me – I was losing ground. My only hope was to catch him as he pulled out of the dive. I turned slightly off his track and got out to one side. I daren't look round and see if anything was following me, because I knew if I took my eyes off him for a second, he would disappear. Somehow or other, they always do against the water. Down and down he went. I'd the awful feeling that the blighter might not pull out in time for me to get a squirt at him. I was doing something near the 500 miles an hour mark – how the hell he hoped to pull out at that speed I'd no idea. He appeared to be absolutely on the water. I expected to see him splash at any second, but somehow I was wrong – he did pull out, slowly, but quite surely. I suppose he looked dead behind him to see if I was still there. That is where the sucker made his first and really last mistake. I was well up on his left and, as near as I could judge, directly up sun as far as he was concerned. I waited a few minutes before

I put in my attack, to make quite sure as to whether he had seen me or not. Apparently not, for he had throttled back and seemed to be taking it quite easy. If he looked back it was only directly behind him. I turned in and gingerly felt for the button. Down I went – still he hadn't seen me – it was the last moment too, for at the second after he saw me my rounds must have hit him. He had been right down on the water-level – I pumped him full. For a few seconds he flew dead straight and suddenly, without any warning, pulled right up and climbed until he reached the vertical – he was finished. Flames were coming from underneath the machine and he was leaving a big trail of black smoke. I didn't try and follow him – when he came down would be time enough, if by any chance he were not finished. He climbed up 500, perhaps 750 feet, then on to his back and straight down into the water – there was a hell of a splash and that was that! Just nothing left. I circled the spot for a while to see if anything came up – not that I really expected anything – but after the bubbles had ceased, all that was left to show for him and his machine was a patch of oil. No good hanging around.

I was some half-way across the Channel – we'd used a hell of a lot of petrol chasing this particular batch and I had to be getting back. I turned towards England and let my thoughts wander, but not too much not to keep a sharp look-out in case some up-to-date unseen Hun pushed in an attack on me. I'd been lucky that time – it had been a pushover, nobody had followed me, I'd got him absolutely off his guard. If only they were all as easy as that. I throttled back to the most economical cruising speed. I hadn't got much petrol left, and if I was not careful I'd have to land and refuel before I could get back to my base. God forbid that I should have to do that! It was just on breakfast-time and I was as ravenous as a wolf.

I wondered what had happened to the others. I wondered if any of them had had any luck, or perhaps, bad luck. Hallo, what's that? Just ahead of me I could see the wake of a fast motor-boat. That meant somebody was down in the drink – I hoped it was one of those bloody Huns. Still, we'd see. I'd take a chance of getting my breakfast this time. I appeared to be the only machine in the sky, so I circled up higher, looking for the tell-tale parachute floating on the water which would give me his approximate position. Sure enough, there it was – the motor-boat was heading away to the right of it; I began circling the spot hoping that they would understand what I meant, but somehow the nitwits didn't. I dived down at them, making a mental note of the position of the parachute, circled them and flew back to the parachute and again circled. Ah, they understood – thank God for that! I might still make base without having to refuel – yes, it was perfectly all right, they were heading straight at him. I could see the pilot swimming towards them.

Just as I reached land, I turned round once and took a quick look – yes, the boat had stopped – they must be picking him up now. Poor devil, I bet he didn't feel too good, most probably on an empty stomach too, and I knew the Channel is none too warm so early in the morning.

Within a few minutes I was back over my base. Another machine was just landing, so I did a circuit. Then down I went. As I taxied in to the dispersal, I quickly counted the machines – ah, well, perhaps they hadn't all landed yet –

yes, there was another one coming in now. I stopped the engine and climbed out: as I did so, the crew and armourers leapt on the machine. I hadn't fired very much, only about 115 per gun, but I was pretty short of petrol – only seven gallons left. I told the crew what had happened as they refuelled the machine, then wandered off towards the Dispersal Hut. There were still three who hadn't landed. No good worrying about them, I'd to get breakfast and be back at readiness as quickly as possible. Apparently to-day, like the last four, was going to be a busy one. What couldn't I do to one of those pre-war breakfasts! Lashings of bacon, eggs and fried bread with plenty of hot sweet coffee – not to mention several rounds of toast well covered with good butter and marmalade.

Just as we were half-way through breakfast, a message came through that we needn't hurry. Things had died down for the time being and we could take it easy; we'd be called when necessary. Nevertheless, we all ate our breakfast as quickly as possible; one never knew how soon it might be necessary. I was just getting up to go, when "Sleepy," our Intelligence Officer, came in and said two of them had landed at other aerodromes to refuel as they had had long chases across the Channel but there was still no news of Starkey. Apparently our net bag for this first trip was five, and as Starkey could not still be in the air, we presumed he was missing, unless by some odd chance he happened to be the bloke that I found swimming for it.

Butch had not fared so well in this show. He'd had a quick squirt at one bloke and before he could get another one in, somebody took a swipe at him. It had been quite a close shave, for he'd got five holes drilled in the fuselage just behind the cockpit. In his efforts to get out of the Hun's way, he lost sight of his original target and his present attacker, and when he had stopped doing his small circles found himself sitting up there all alone. There wasn't much more that he could do, so he just had to come home. Ginger, on the other hand, had had a fair crack at his bloke and chased him nearly the whole way over to France. He got in five or six bursts and used all his ammunition. He left his Hun making for France with a trail of white smoke coming out of him. He didn't think that the Jerry would have a chance of making it, but even so, if he didn't make the coast, he'd almost certainly be picked up by their Rescue Service.

Well, not a bad start for the day; if we kept going along those lines, we'd be doing fine.

I dashed along to my room and had gotten half-way through my shave when the call to readiness came. I wiped the lather off the other side of my face and rushed out of the mess, only just in time to catch the transport. There was still two blokes missing, but we couldn't wait for them. We roared off to the Dispersal and as we got there, the telephone orderly shouted that we were to take off at once. Yes, things were going to be hot to-day. I clambered into the machine and strapped myself in tightly. The other two had just arrived. They would be late off, but they'd make it, thank heavens! Even one missing makes a hell of a difference when you're going up to meet almost inevitably very much heavier odds.

It was the same patrol. Apparently the Hun had sent some more machines over, but they were flying much higher this time. The sun was fairly high and the grass was as near as damn it bone dry – all the dew had disappeared. As we taxied out, the dust began to rise. Yes, it was exactly the same as yesterday, and the day before. We lined up into position. Where the hell was that other fellow? There should have been ten, somehow there were only nine. Again we roared off, and as we circled the aerodrome, I looked down and saw one of the machines still in its dispersal position. There was a small knot of men standing around it. Something had gone wrong. Then, suddenly, another machine started taxi-ing out. Good fellow! He'd been able to switch his kit into another machine and get away, and by taxi-ing at break-neck speed, he caught us as we threw out the "grappling hooks" and gained height. The clouds had become just a bit thicker now and, when we got well up above them, I saw that they extended way out across the Channel. As I looked down, so I had the impression of looking at a lovely piece of slightly red-tinted cotton-wool which had been laid across that plasticine model of the south-east coast of England. Butch and Ginger were flying beautifully, but what was that damn fellow in front of us doing? Why the devil couldn't he get into position? He was wobbling all over the place, upsetting us. In spite of the strict orders about R/T silence, I had to tell him either to keep position or to get to hell out of it. For a few minutes more he wobbled and swayed, then returned to normal and got in close and stayed there like a rock. I felt sorry I'd cursed him. He'd most probably been having trouble with some of his controls or got one of his straps caught up in the tail trimmer. Still, it had been bloody annoying.

In spite of the fact that it'd been quite warm when we took off, it was still pretty darned cold up here. When we got to thirty-two thousand, we levelled out. We'd flown north-east in order to get the best results out of the sun, but it didn't much matter now, for the Hun had it in his favour the whole time. We turned south and again started out across the Channel; then, about mid-Channel, we turned again and started sweeping down the Channel. Yes, there they were, the blighters – way over on our right we could see the smoke trails. They were high, all right, most probably thirty-four thousand. We didn't turn towards them at once. We started climbing and hoped to heavens that we'd be able to cut them off. Somehow or other, I didn't think we could. They were travelling at a hell of a speed and we'd still to make up at least two thousand feet. After what seemed hours (but was most probably only three or four minutes) we were almost up to them, but they were still above us. We had started leaving smoke trails ourselves now, so they couldn't help but see us. We started turning: it was no good, we couldn't intercept them before they passed over us, so we turned and flew along on a parallel course and, with a bit of luck, they'd come down to have a pot at us and we'd get away without too much damage. Not a bit of it. The yellow rats kept on flying up there, about a thousand feet above us. We daren't push our noses up and try and make up that thousand feet, because it would have reduced our speed too much and made us far too easy a target. We were climbing maybe a hundred feet a minute – certainly not more. With luck we might be up on their level by the time we got somewhere near France. The chances were that they'd start increasing height themselves. Suddenly, two of the Huns dived and took a quick spray at us, climbing back out of reach before we could do anything about it. Oh ho! so that was the game, was it? Quickly we split, one flight going on either side of 'em and just waiting for the next pair to come down. Sure enough they did, and as they did so a pair from the other flight turned across in an effort to catch them before they could climb up again, but it wasn't any good – they were wily, as well as yellow. We'd almost reached the French coast by now and we'd had quite a long chase, preceded by a fast climb. We couldn't afford to hang around as there was no telling that there might be another formation of Huns coming up to chase us back, in which case we'd need every ounce of petrol we had, so we turned round and made for home without having fired a shot!

As far as we were concerned, there was quite a lull in the morning's work. An hour had elapsed since we refuelled, and everybody was lolling around outside the dispersal. The sun was beating down on us and with all my flying kit I was really feeling much too hot, but I daren't take any of it off, for I knew perfectly well that above thirty thousand feet I'd just freeze to death if I didn't keep it on.

Two or three of the blokes were dozing again. Butch and I had just discussed a few of yesterday's events and I was going to sit back for a doze myself when young Ginger came over to me and told me he was putting in for a few days' leave, as his sister was getting married. What did I think were the chances of his getting it? As far as I could see, there wasn't any reason why he couldn't get it. He was sorry to have to rat on us like this just when we were so busy, but he really wanted to go, if he could possibly get the time off. Anyway, it'd most probably do him a lot of good; he was looking tired and for his nineteen years he'd been doing a hell of a sight too much.

I began to feel restless. What was up with the Hun today? He had started off so well. I was surprised that we hadn't been kept busy, but maybe it was the lull before the storm.

I shambled over to the telephone and had a few words with Ops. Apparently, there was absolutely nothing doing – not even a "Jim Crow" about. Out I went again, into the sun. Might as well get sunburnt as not. Somehow, one always felt better when one looked in the mirror in the morning and saw a decently sunburnt face. The green pallor left after the party of the night before didn't show up so much, and although you might feel like death, you certainly didn't look it, which is always some sort of a consolation. I lay down in the long grass and used a chock as a headrest, closed my eyes and let my mind wander. It was amazing to think that it was just over a year ago that I was in Germany. What fun I'd had in spite of the Nazi regime, and on the whole, what a friendly bunch they'd been. Strange, too, having as many friends as I had over there, I now felt not the slightest compunction about shooting any of 'em except maybe that lovely blonde; she was after all "un objet d'art."

Old Sleepy, our Intelligence Officer, padded round the corner of the Dispersal Hut – "Whatcher, chaps. I hear Starkey is all right. He had to bale-out and got himself lost in a wood. The Home Guard treated him with the utmost suspicion – they thought he was skulking in the wood, instead of trying to find his way out. However, he's all right – really none the worse for wear – in fact, he's quite pleased with himself, because he'll now become a member of the Caterpillar Club. If I'm not mistaken, it has always been one of his ambitions." Having delivered himself of this piece of information, Old Sleepy wandered away rather aimlessly towards the aerodrome. Nice old devil! but really quite a puzzle. One just hadn't any idea what he was going to do or say next. Come to think of it, I don't really think even he did. He did his job magnificently, but there's no doubt about it, the rest of his life was just one dream after another – nothing ever seemed to rouse him. Even that day when those cheeky blighters came over and dropped some half-dozen eggs or so on the place, all he did was pad out of his office and want to know "What all the noise was about?" As he disappeared round a distant hedge, my mind switched back to the Hun again. Somehow, one almost always thinks about either the Hun or the next meal, sometimes about blokes who had come or gone. One would go over in one's mind exactly what had happened in the last two or three combats, try to find out exactly what it was that you'd done wrong and allowed that bloke to take a pot at you; why you hadn't been able to shake him off your tail sooner; or, perhaps, why had it taken so much ammunition to pull that last bloke down. It'd been a different proposition when I was flying Hurricanes and had been shooting up the Hun bombers. There's no doubt about it, those 109's were very much more tricky.

Ops. have just been on the phone to say that there was nothing happening. What the hell could be wrong with the Hun to-day? This was most unusual. I dozed off. One never really sleeps very soundly when at readiness. Then suddenly I was brought to my senses by a yell – we're off again! Everybody was dashing about – the usual scene was taking place just before the take-off – I felt drowsy and very much disinclined to go and chase the Hun or be chased by him. However, off we went. As usual, we clambered up to thirty thousand, and on the way up I couldn't help thinking about the lunch that we were leaving behind, because I noticed now that it was almost lunch-time. Most probably it wouldn't be a good one, but it would be hot, had we been able to get it just now. As it was, it'd be a good hour before we could get back to the mess.

We wheeled away to south-east. Apparently the break we'd had this morning was indeed the lull before the storm, for the Hun seemed to be sending in sweep after sweep across the coast – most probably only fighters, but you never can tell: might be the odd bomber formations slipped in between. We hadn't been at thirty thousand for more than a minute when we saw the first one. Were we in luck? It was about 2,000 feet below and dead ahead. We were just preparing to dive into the attack when, by the grace of God, we saw the formation above and up-sun! Those wily devils had laid a trap but we hadn't fallen. Instead we wheeled into the sun and went straight at 'em. They were only a matter of a thousand feet above us and our move was so unexpected that we rather caught them napping. They broke up as we got to them, and dived like the frightened bunch of rats that they were. One of them most certainly never pulled out. I couldn't follow him, but he was on fire as he went and we were still in pretty good formation. We wheeled and chased the other bunch that had been below us. They had turned round and were on their way back, thinking that the people up-sun had taken care of us. They were stooging along most probably thinking of their lunch also – but not for long! They literally didn't see us and had no idea that we'd started our attack until three of 'em went down, but we no sooner started the attack than we ourselves were again being attacked. Another wave had arrived overhead at least some good two to three thousand feet above us and they came hurtling down at us straight out of the sun. The lads rallied beautifully in spite of the fact that we'd been surprised. Half of them turned up and met the diving Hun (there's nothing like putting on a bold face when you're in a tight corner – the Hun simply won't stand up to it – if you show fight, he turns tail every single time). This time, however, it was too late for 'em to turn tail: they simply couldn't stop their attack and they were met by four Spits. coming straight at 'em with guns going. I couldn't see what happened to them after that; in fact, I'd been lucky to be able to watch that much of the combat, for I was just closing in on another Hun and was getting all set to give him a burst, when I felt the judder of some Hun's slugs going into my machine. Next moment a cannon shell burst on the starboard wing root, and at the same instant there was a damned unpleasant feeling in my leg. As all this happened I'd been pressing the tit, and by some strange coincidence the Hun in front of me broke in the same direction that I broke away myself. I just followed him around and got in another quick burst, which sent him down out of control. The little bastard was still on my tail. I had to shake him off before I could do anything more. My leg was beginning to hurt quite a lot. There was no two ways about it, I'd been stung again and if I wasn't careful the blighter on my tail would put the finishing touches to it. I tightened the turn-up and could see him vainly struggling to follow me round, but it wasn't any good – I was turning quite easily inside him. If he'd stick, I'd be able to get on to his tail, but just as I thought he was going to be sucker enough to stay put, another Spit. came to my assistance. The Hun must have been so engrossed in trying to catch me up that he couldn't have seen the other bloke coming. It must have been a direct hit in the petrol tank, because he just blew to bits!

I straightened out for an instant to watch him go down, then as I looked round again for something to shoot at, I saw a Spit. hurtling down at me. Was the fellow going to take a pot at me? I yelled at him over the R/T but he came straight on down. I turned in underneath him, but he tried to follow. I cursed the pilot for being a bloody fool, but it's difficult to tell in the heat of battle what a machine is if you cannot see it properly. Hell! I'd done the same myself, so what!

The leg of my trousers had begun to stick to my leg and I found that I couldn't put the full pressure of my foot on the rudder bar, but I still had some ammunition, and I thought I might be able to make good if only I could tag on to another Hun in time.

The sky was a whirling mass of machines. I could see four parachutes drifting down slowly below me and there was a machine streaking down over on the right in flames – the pilot dangling on his parachute about 3,000 feet above. Just at that moment I caught sight of another Spitfire. He'd got a couple of devils on his tail. By luck I happened to be up-sun of them, so I turned and sprayed the two of 'em, but not quite in time, I'm afraid. There was an explosion and the Spitfire came to bits . . . it must have been a direct hit in the engine. As I sprayed them, still at fairly long range, the rearmost one in line broke away and went into a vertical dive. I think he was just getting out of the way, but the leader must have been too interested in the Spit. he'd just blown apart, for he started slowly circling and watching it going down. Now was my chance! I got up close to him and slightly underneath him – then I pulled the stick back, pressed the tit. There was an explosion and he burst into a sheet of flame from the cockpit to the tail. The machine levelled out and the pilot started to climb out. I gave another short burst: the pilot seemed to straighten up in the cockpit and then sagged over the side. That was one Hun less.

In the meantime, I'd made that unforgivable mistake of not watching my own tail. The machine shuddered and there was an explosion, the hood fell to bits, and my instruments began to fall apart. Petrol began gushing into the cockpit. I stamped my left foot down on the rudder and pulled the stick back hard and then reversed the process and streaked down towards the ground. The petrol was getting in my eyes, I couldn't see a damn thing. Thank God, it hadn't caught fire. I was soaked to the skin and my neck was hurting like hell. I expect I'd been hit again, but by now all I was concerned with was getting out of that machine just as quickly as I could. There were only two instruments on the panel that were working; I suddenly realised that my right arm didn't seem to be there, and although I exerted all my strength of will, I couldn't make my hand pull the stick back. I realised that in spite of the coldness of the petrol, the back of my arm felt hot and sticky. I whipped my goggles off and tried rubbing the petrol out of my eyes, but that only made it worse. I pushed them back again and getting my left hand on the stick I began to pull out of the dive. I'd no idea what height I was at, for I'd been going down for what seemed an age and I must be damn' close to the deck by now. My neck and leg were stinging like hell, as the petrol got into the open flesh. I felt strangely faint. I whipped my oxygen mask off and the next moment got a mouthful of petrol. That was no good. I couldn't possibly put the mask back, and yet every time I breathed I stood a good chance of getting a mouthful of petrol or some up my nostrils. I opened the hood and pushed my face out over the side and hoped for the best. I began to think a bit more clearly now and realised how lucky I was that the machine was not on fire. If it'd caught fire and even if I baled-out, I would have been burnt to a cinder, my clothes and parachute being by now absolutely saturated in petrol. I was still feeling faint and a strong feeling of sickness began to creep over me. The question was, could I land this sieve of mine or would it be better to bale-out? I hadn't the vaguest idea where I was now. I'd been going round in circles for about five minutes trying to clear my head and reach some rational decision. I felt for my map, but couldn't find it. I'd have to do something damn quick, otherwise the petrol would conk out and there was always the chance that the machine might catch on fire at any moment. I was south of my base. I reckoned up my chances of being able to get back to base before the petrol ran out. Of course it would be ideal to get the machine back almost in one piece, but at the rate the petrol was pouring into the cockpit, I thought it better not to take the chance. If the engine did conk out half-way there, the chances of getting her down in a field in one piece would be very much against me.

Sticking my head well over the side, the tears caused by the petrol soon began to clear and I was again able to see the ground more or less clearly. There were quite a number of possible fields for me to get into, but damn me, if they were not all barricaded against the invasion. Here was a pretty pickle! What the hell was I going to do now? I flew around for a couple of minutes, looking at one very big field and decided that, with luck, I could land in between all the obstructions. I made a careful note of the line of approach, pushed my wheels down and the flaps. I was determined to get the machine down in as much one piece as possible. Then, I started throttling back with a nasty feeling that sparks, which usually occurs as one throttles back, might set the machine alight. If they did, there wasn't a hope in hell. A pity if it ended like that, having gotten away with so much already. The only thing to do was to cut the switches and hope to God that my judgment of the height was good enough. I held my breath. I was over-shooting. A quick side slip, which was all to the good because I could see all that was happening in front of me, and we landed with a hell of a thud! I jammed on the brakes and worked frantically to keep her straight. Poles were whizzing by on either side: a car loomed up, but my wing-tip just cleared it. Gradually we slowed. Then I was brought up with a tremendous jerk – I had gone head-on into an old car, but fortunately it did nothing more than snap one of the blades off the propeller! Hell, but that was a shaky do! I just sat in the cockpit for a few moments, really not quite sure what to do for quite a couple of minutes. I just didn't know. Then the pain in my neck, arm and leg roused me into action. I felt absolutely frozen with my bath in petrol, so I started climbing out. My right arm had gradually come back to life and was hurting quite a bit. As I clambered out of the cockpit, half hopping and half sliding, and got on to the ground, the Home Guard, and I should think the whole population of the local village, arrived on the scene. There were too many people smoking. Petrol was still pouring out of the machine and they wanted to clamber all over it with lighted cigarettes and pipes. However, they were very good about it all and the local cop. and two of the Home Guard soon made every one keep a safe distance from the machine. The trouble was I wanted a smoke myself, but I daren't have one because my tunic was still saturated with the petrol. I found I could walk all right, but my neck felt pretty stiff and my arm was still pretty useless. Leaving the local cop. and Home Guard in charge, I was whisked away by a local ambulance party to a neighbouring First-Aid Centre. I must say I felt the need of a little attention right then. What I wanted most was a cup of very hot and very sweet tea, and I felt sure that, rationing or not, I was going to get it this time.

We arrived at the Centre. I was marched into the operating theatre and was horrified (not to mention scared stiff) to see no less than seven females, got up in all sorts of white gadgets, with an eager look on their faces. Now I don't mind a doctor, although I know quite a few are hard-hearted devils who probe into you and pull things out, but when you see the seven eager faces of amateur first-aid workers, it is enough to send a shiver down anybody's spine, and I made a solemn little vow as I went in that all they would do would be to put a dressing on and leave it at that. Not a bit of it. I was invited to lie on the operating table, while they neatly sliced my trousers leg and sleeve from end to end. (Good-bye, dear tunic, it was the bitter end.) Instruments were produced from all round. I felt that a major operation was about to take place, so I sat up and voiced my feelings. After a lot of argument, they agreed that they would only put on a dressing, which I must say they did extremely efficiently. It was not until I was being washed and dressed that I realised that my face was cut about too. The bridge of my nose had been skinned by a flying piece of glass. My neck had cannon-shell splinters in it; my arm had pulled up something like a spent bullet and, of course, my leg had quite a few bits of cannon-shell splinters – none of it very bad, but just bad enough to make it all unpleasant.

By the time they'd finished tinkering about with me, the most junior had done a wonderful job in producing not just a cup, but a whole bowlful of delicious sweet tea. I was not quite sure about the bowl, because it came off the operating table, but I guess, being a First Aid Post, it had been sterilized.

After telephoning my unit and letting them know I was O.K. and a round of thanks to all seven of my Ministering Angels, I went back and took a really good look at the machine. No doubt about it, I'd had a lucky escape and I don't intend to have any more close shaves like that. In future, I'm damn well going to have eyes in the back of my head and make sure the Hun does not catch me napping. I'd two cannon shells in one wing, one in the other, and one in the fuselage, and seven bullet holes had punctured the lower petrol tank. I came close to buying a packet that time! Never mind, I was still alive – by God, I'll pay them out for this! After doing one or two things to the machine and unloading the guns (so that none of the special friends of the local Guards who were permitted to climb into the machine would blow somebody else's head off) I was given a lift to the nearest station. I must say I felt a bit strange. I had my parachute and flying kit over my arm, my trousers leg ripped up to the knee and my right sleeve ripped up to the shoulder – bandages all over the place and a very dirty face. Then the trouble started. They didn't want to let me travel on the train because I couldn't pay for the ticket. Like a fool I hadn't even got a penny on me! However, with a lot of argument, I got into the train just before it left. It was a corridor train and the news went round like a flash that there was some peculiar specimen caged up in a first-class carriage by himself. I wouldn't swear to it, but I think everybody, including the guard, paraded up and down outside my compartment having a look at me! I regret to say that I was dim enough not to remember about such things as window blinds, but the guard must have had a kindly feeling towards "the mess" sitting in the corner, for he came in and suggested that he lock the doors and pull the blinds.

On reaching the nearest station to my unit, I dived into a taxi and was driven home – well, to the sick quarters. The doc. took one look at me and said, "Hum – sorry, old boy, we'll have to take some of this out," so with another cup of hot tea, this time with all the sugar I wanted, plus a liberal ration of rum, I stretched out and the brute got down to work. It is a funny thing about these doctors. They always tell you, "Now it won't hurt," and "It's for your own good," but I can't tell you how much more painful it was having it taken out than pushed in!

Anyway, after a long time of juggling about with probes

and forceps they got all the big chunks out. I reckoned that was enough for one day, and as they put the dressing on, was planning what sort of party I'd be having, when dammit, the doctor said I'd have to get to bed! That was too much. Normally, I'm very amenable to discipline, but hell, not after to-day. Ale, and strong ale, was indicated, and besides which, I'd heard that we'd had a pretty good success that day (up to date, we'd bagged seventeen, and only two missing – unfortunately, of the two Ginger was one). It took me a long time to persuade the doc. that putting me to bed would be absolutely futile, so he let me roam off to the mess for a meal. After my lunch-cum-tea, I ambled down to the dispersal and had a "natter" with the blokes. Nobody had seen poor old Ginger go, but they found his machine and it'd dug itself in deep. There were three other wounded besides myself, but fortunately, only one seriously. It looked as if he would have to lose his right leg: a bloody shame, because he was one of the best three-quarters we ever had. On the other hand, better that than pushing up daisies.

From six o'clock onwards there was not much doing – in fact, there was only one stooge patrol, and nothing happened on it. I guess the Hun had had enough for that day.

As soon as the blokes were released, did we go out on a party! I don't really remember the end of that party – I had too good a time.

INTRODUCING PICKLE

Pickle is a character. He is just twenty, short, thin and looks half starved, but he can and does eat just as much as any of us. His hair is all over the place – I don't think even glue would keep it down, especially that funny tuft that always falls over his right eye. You couldn't fail to pick him out anywhere because he walks twice as fast as anybody else and kind of leans forward to it as if he were pushing against a head wind. He talks fast and in spasms; it is no good trying to pick up a conversation half-way through, as by the time you have digested the first few words he has finished the whole sentence.

The more work you give Pickle the happier he is; in fact, I can safely say that you cannot possibly give him too much. He does everything the same way – at top speed.

There is another peculiarity about Pickle. When I first met him he could take a half can of beer and that was that. With a year's training he now manages about one and a half cans.

He's a most amazing individual on a party. He dashes about at his usual high speed, dances, nabbles the bogle, but after a time, and having drunk his normal quota of booze-wine, he quietly disappears. When the party is over all one has to do is look around in the quiet corners to find him peacefully sleeping in an arm-chair, a straight-back chair, or sometimes even on the floor – not drunk, just tired.

Pickle's Story

It was the beginning of the "blitz" when I joined the squadron, and after about twenty operational hours' flying and never having seen a Jerry, I was rather browned-off, but I knew the day was coming, and when it came I had one of the most exciting times of my life.

We were stationed at an aerodrome on the east coast, our work consisting mainly of convoy patrols and sometimes an interception patrol. We slept at our Dispersal Points, because we came into readiness at dawn, which was about 4.30, and usually did not finish until 11.30 with an hour off for breakfast, lunch and dinner.

One bright summer's afternoon our section was ordered off to patrol the East Coast from Point X to Point Y. We had climbed to 25,000 feet when I sighted an aircraft flying towards us about 3,000 feet above. At once I informed the leader I would lead the section towards it. As soon as he saw the aircraft, which we identified as a DO. 215, he ordered the section to prepare to attack.

The section climbed above the DO. 215 and the leader put us into line astern. We then dived, giving the DO. 215 an astern attack, and as he closed the range the rear gunner of the E/A opened fire, which was not very accurate. Number two then went into line astern of the leader and I followed, but slightly to the starboard, when the leader broke away to port. Then number two attacked; by this time another gunner had taken his position in the tail of the E/A and number two received a hell of return fire. When he had finished firing the E/A's port engine was on fire and its fuselage had had pieces knocked off. I then attacked myself, opening fire at about 250 yards. Suddenly the E/A starboard engine caught fire: all the oil was thrown back by the slip-stream on my windscreen, and as I was blinded for a few seconds, immediately I put on full left rudder, at the same time I pushed the control column over to the left and did not level out until I had lost 2,000 feet.

As the hood was covered with oil I decided to open it, and much to my surprise found the DO. 215 was about ten feet away on my starboard side. The rear gunner played merry hell into my machine with his machine-gun before it was possible to break away. The hood departed and the wireless was put out of action and I decided that no "Jerry" was going to get away with this, so I attacked again, but this time I opened fire at 100 yards, not stopping until I noticed that my glycol was on fire. Under these conditions I had to break upwards to gain as much height as possible, which would allow extra time to study my position before force-landing.

I had 5,000 feet between me and the sea, the coast was about ten miles away, my engine had cut out, the glycol was on fire, and my wireless out of action. Should I bale-out, or should I try and glide as near the coast as possible? And then I noticed a lightship below me. In a flash I had made up my mind that I would try and land my machine in the sea by the side of the lightship rather than bale-out as the wind might carry me farther out to sea.

Having decided on this line of action, I glided towards the lightship, thinking my troubles were over. Were they hell! Actually they had only just started. The sea was quite rough and I could not see anything to tell me which direction the wind was blowing from, so I had to take a chance and I wondered what would happen if my airspeed indicator failed to work on the way down. I am now sure that had it failed I would not be here to write this line. I believe that this was the only instrument that I looked at all the way down. I could not see anybody on the lightship. By this time I was only about 500 feet up and I found great trouble in judging how far I was off the sea, and instead of pancaking the machine on the surface it stalled, the left wing dropped and hit the sea with a hell of a crash, and I was thrown forward.

This was the last thing I remembered until I recovered consciousness a few seconds later. I was still in the machine, which was sinking rapidly, and the water was by now up to my neck. As I took a deep breath I was dragged under by the machine. After struggling I freed the harness and tried to push myself clear of the machine, but my parachute caught on a jagged edge of the torn fuselage. After a hefty kick I managed to get clear of the machine, and as I had been under the water for quite a time now, I was beginning to feel dizzy and I had visions of my name on the R.A.F. casualty list, "Killed in action." Also a telegram arriving at home to say I had been bumped off. Suddenly all this thinking stopped. At last I had reached the surface and I took a deep breath and once again I felt normal. The sea was rough and I could see damn all, but at last I saw the lightship about 200 yards away up-current, and therefore started to swim. After about 50 yards I realised that I still had my parachute on and I had forgotten to blow up my "Mae West."

After discarding my parachute, I again made for the lightship, but my shoes seemed to drag along so I took them off, once again remembering that I had forgotten to blow up my "Mae West." This did not seem to have any effect, and I noticed that the air was coming out of the side where I had two little holes. Hell! they had been made by a bullet and only just missed my body. I think I would have died of shock had I not been so cold. By now I was beginning to wonder if I would ever reach the lightship; I did not seem to get any nearer and I was feeling the effects of my submarine act.

The current was rather strong and I was getting weak. As the lightship was still deserted I concluded it was automatic, but suddenly the lightship became alive with men dashing about, so I yelled like hell and in about a minute a boat was lowered and started to come towards me and I just waited. When it got within ten yards I heard the seaman calling, "We're coming, mate," but another of my rescuers was not so sure. He said, "Its a bloody Hun, Bill. Give me the boathook just in case he gets annoying." Bill answered, "No! He came in a Spitfire, Curly"; and as the boat got nearer I saw a tough-looking seaman standing in the stern with a vicious looking boathook in his left hand. Suddenly I sprang to life and yelled a few words of "old-fashioned English." It worked like a miracle. The seaman dropped his boathook (maybe he was shocked) and they cheered. The tough-looking seaman once again had something in his left hand. "Ah! a bottle of rum," and I needed it.

After the Trinity House men had got me aboard the lightship they took all particulars and sent out a W/T message to shore. I then stripped all my wet clothes off and had a bath. By this time I was beginning to feel seasick so I dashed to the side, but forgot about it when I noticed a destroyer coming towards the lightship, also two other light craft just arriving from the harbour ten miles away. Considering they arrived fifteen minutes after I had pancaked on the water I have no fear of rotting in the sea in future, when I know that we have such an efficient Navy to look after us.

After thanking every one on the lightship and by request handing over my "Mae West," flying suit, lapel badges, and many other oddments as souvenirs, I left. The destroyer offered me chocolate and cigarettes. At last I was on my way back home. When the lifeboat was alongside it was attached to the slings and hauled on board. As soon as the lifeboat had left the water and still being hauled on board, the destroyer was under way. Once on board the destroyer I was taken to the bridge and the Commander shook hands with me and I again gave my particulars. He then gave me his cabin, and the ship's doc. had a good look at me and much to my surprise decided to stitch my head. I had no idea it was cut, and he gave me a few injections. When I had been lying down for about ten minutes I felt very tired and went to sleep. At ten I woke up feeling extremely unsafe, and in the distance I heard a gun fire and then another. Gradually the guns got nearer and nearer, until there was a hell of a crash above me, so I sat up suddenly, hit my head on the deck above, and collapsed on my bed again. I was sure by now that the ship was being attacked or had hit a mine or something. Then the door opened and in walked the doc. and informed me that it was only a 4-

inch gun on deck practising. The other gunfire was from destroyers in line astern behind ours.

We put into Sheerness at 06.00 hours the following morning and it had been arranged that I should be transferred to a Hospital at Chatham at 10.00 hours. At 08.00 hours I got up and had some breakfast. Afterwards I sat in a deck chair on the quarter-deck, but at 09.30 the air-raid warning sounded and about 100 enemy aircraft came from the south, but the A/A fire was so tremendous that the E/A were completely split up and only a few managed to dive-bomb the harbour, and for the next five minutes the noise was colossal – whistles of failing bombs and crashes as bombs exploded in the water and 4-inch A/A opened fire: all this mingled with the rat-tat of machine-guns and pompoms. The destroyer seemed to rock once or twice when the bombs fell near, but nothing was sunk and ten E/A fell into the estuary.

I was taken to hospital by a smashing Wren and put to bed for five days. The hospital staff were tremendous and my nurse was a wizard type. The naval officers were the best types possible and for five days I had the most enjoyable time imaginable, but I was getting homesick for my squadron. I had already heard that they had moved farther into the heart of the "blitz."

The leader and No. 2 had not seen me crash and were very surprised to find that I had not returned, and nobody received any message until three hours after, but when it arrived they gathered that I was on a cruiser and would not be back for a few weeks. The C.O. was very surprised when I arrived back, but he would not let me fly. The doc. then sent me on two weeks' leave, which did not do me much good as I stayed in London for a week and then I returned to the squadron, but the C.O. sent me away again as I still could not fly. I spent most of my time at the pictures as there was nothing else to do. My relatives were so good to me that I got fed up with them, and was relieved to get back to the squadron. I arrived back at the squadron and heard that the DO. 215 had crashed a few miles from the lightship.

The "blitz" was at its height when I returned. The squadron looked different with D.F.C.s and parts of ME. 109's littered all over the Dispersal Point. But all I wanted to do was to get my own back.

The first time up after my last episode there were six of us on patrol when we sighted about thirty ME. 109's about 5,000 feet above us, so we climbed to attack, but we were attacked by thirty ME. 109's from behind. I was attacked by six at once, but after being hit three times I managed to get away by going into a spin.

After spinning from 25,000 feet to 5,000 feet I pulled out. All the time I expected to get a few more bullets into my machine because I did not realise that ME. 109's do not follow Spitfires and Hurricanes once they go into a spin or dive, and much to my surprise an ME. 109 was about 400 yards ahead of me flying south. I closed to 200 yards and opened fire. It dived and the last I saw was when it entered the cloud at 2,000 feet with glycol flames pouring out of the radiator, but I could only claim it as damaged. When I got back to the base two of the boys had not arrived back but they arrived later, each having shot down an Me. 109. The total score for this fight was six 109's shot down, three probably shot down, and four damaged. Our only casualty was my machine, which was repaired within an hour.

After a few more flights over London and the south coast I began to feel at home fighting 109's.

On the 10th October the squadron was ordered to take off, but unfortunately I was held up, so I had to take off by myself. After searching for the squadron I called up the ground station and they told me that the squadron were having a fight, and if I went down to the coast I might catch something returning home. I climbed to 35,000 feet and waited. At last I saw six ME. 109's in line astern, crossing the coast between Dover and Folkestone. I dived and opened fire. The aim was too high and only warned them that I was attacking. They spread out fanwise, making it very difficult for me to attack any one without having the other five on my tail, so I dived for cloud cover. Once in the cloud I decided to stalk them over the Channel. I hopped in and out of the clouds, gradually catching them up, but I did not realise that by this time I was over Calais until the aircraft rocked and Jerry sent up about 100 A.-A. shells. Unfortunately one piece of shrapnel pierced my radiator and my engine seized up. Wondering if I would have to make another forced-landing in the sea and if so would I be as lucky as last time. Half-way I saw six 109's approaching but fortunately they were being chased by a Spitfire after crossing the coast. I looked for an aerodrome but could not find one, but managed to find a big field. After gliding down to 1,000 feet everything was still under control, but suddenly the cockpit and instruments became covered in thick oil and I could not see at what airspeed I was travelling at. My speed must have been at over 200 m.p.h. as I completely overshot the big field, also smaller ones, and my machine went straight through a hedge, leaving its radiator behind, knocked down four trees, at the same time relieving itself of its starboard wing, and then cartwheeled over a pile of felled trees which unfortunately decided to keep the engine. These little things did not seem to slow the machine down. My tail plane had to catch hold of a tree before the fuselage would consider slowing down, but not quick enough to enable the tail to stay attached to the fuselage.

Once again the rest of the fuselage cartwheeled over a tree and then came to a standstill. For a few seconds I just sat in the remains of my machine and wondered what had happened, but suddenly noticed that the cockpit had caught fire, so I hopped out and ran like hell with my parachute on for the nearest tree. Carefully I looked round the side of the tree. Hell! I could not see a thing out of my right eye. Was I blinded? In a few minutes crowds of people arrived and one person in particular decided that I must have been knocked out and had fallen in the cockpit. He climbed into the machine and lifted the seat up, and to his dismay could not find anybody. When I dashed up and tapped him on the shoulder he must have thought I was a ghost, as he just stared at me and did not say a word for a few seconds, and after that he only said "Good God." By now I was fully convinced that I had been blinded, but it was not so, all that had happened was that I had a beautiful black eye.

When I arrived back at my squadron the "blitz" was practically over. We only had a few more fights but nothing exciting happened. We as a squadron had shot down over sixty enemy aircraft, another sixty probably, and a good many damaged, for the loss of only seven pilots, two of whom were killed accidentally.

The boys are still waiting for the next "blitz." A good many of us have had experience but these experiences do not affect us like they affect our parents, who are worrying a lot more than us and I suppose they will start worrying as soon as I get shot down again. I will now close this line as I have been ordered off again to search for a Hun coming in our direction.

NOTE.—I did not get him. He ran back home.

EDITOR'S NOTE

Since writing these lines our gallant little Pickle has, alas! been killed whilst flying on active service. "Per Ardua Ad Astra."

INTRODUCING CLAUDE

Claude was of medium height, well built and inclined to tubbiness. He was always well turned out. He had one of those cheerful smiles and happy dispositions which are a joy to meet, and I can't recall a single occasion on which his cheerfulness deserted him.

He knew more about Spitfires than any of the other peelows, as he had been with Supermarines before he joined the R.A.F. This knowledge of his machine and his keenness as a pilot often came out in discussions, as he was able to answer most queries, which he did invariably with the aid of model machines.

A most unassuming bloke with lots of what it takes, a good type on parties, with a great sense of humour.

Claude's Story

IT WAS just after the wonderful evacuation of our army from Dunkirk that I joined my first fighter squadron. I was particularly thrilled, because I had applied from the very first interview with my commanding officer at Initial Training Wing and throughout my training to be allowed to fly Spitfire fighters. Here I will just say that before the war I built and serviced Spitfires as a representative of Messrs. Vickers Armstrong, Ltd., hence my desire to become a pilot of one of the aircraft I really loved.

After my training I was posted to a Hurricane Operational Training Unit; this meant usually that I would never see a Spitfire squadron, or, I would like to add, that's what I thought! When I was posted it was to a Spitfire squadron. I felt on top of the world: rather like a schoolboy who had just received his first prize at the annual sports day.

I did quite a lot of flying as soon as I joined my squadron, practising attacks and generally getting the handling of Spitfires taped. I went to bed one evening, non-operational, but still hoping for the day when I would be classed as an operational pilot, and strut around the Dispersal with a "Mae West" on and my crew and machine ready to take off at a moment's notice. The following morning I was wakened at about 03.15 hours by an airman, who said, "Get up, Sarge, you are operational and wanted on readiness at 03.45 hours." I was out of bed like a shot, for my time had come to really do something.

Unfortunately nothing happened that morning. However, in the afternoon we got the call to take off and patrol a convoy going through the Straits of Dover. All was quiet for a while, but just as we were getting fed up with pottering up and down the ships, a message came over the R/T telling us the Huns were about to attack the convoy. Everything seemed to happen very quickly after that. Before I realised the position, there was a tremendous dog-fight under way. The first I knew was tracer bullets whizzing past my hood, whereupon I acted very quickly. Forgetting all my training, I pulled the aeroplane into a steep, shuddering left turn and climbed into the cloud. As I emerged from the cloud I saw the Hun just below me and recognised his aeroplane as an ME. 109E. Here I had the advantage and went down on him from behind. He saw me and pulled up into the cloud. I waited below, as I thought he would come out again. Next I saw his aeroplane as a dark shadow coming slowly into a vertical climb. Got my sights on the dim form of the 109 and fired my eight guns. It was the first time I had fired all eight guns of a fighter. The result was amazing: the ME. 109 just fell out of the cloud like a brick. But the 109 was not the only one to fall out of the sky, for at the same time my aeroplane stalled and started a violent spin to the left. It only did about one and a half turns before I got it out. Diving down to get some speed again, I saw more splashes in the water, after which there seemed to be a series of water spouts all at once. Bombs! thought I. By this time I had forgotten all about my ME. 109 duel, having seen nothing more of him.

My feelings by this time were a queer mixture of fright, delight at having beaten a 109, and amazement, when I saw the long thin fuselage of a Dornier 215. As I closed up I noticed the dark olive-green camouflage of the Hun bomber and the large black crosses on the white background. The sea was misty, which made the greenish-looking bomber very difficult to see. Before attacking, as there were no mirrors fitted to our fighters, I did a quick turn to the left and right to see that there was nothing on my tail. I opened fire at about 250 yards, meeting with considerable opposition from the rear gunner. I got in a good burst before breaking away. I made rather a mess of my break-away and got some bullets from what I think was a *blister* gun in his port side. When I got straight again there was nothing in sight, so I decided to go home to our forward base and land. On the way I took stock of the result of my first combat. The position to me looked grim, for I was full of holes and pieces were ripping off the wings as I flew. Result, a probable 109 and damaged Dornier. As I was doing the circuit I saw that my airspeed indicator registered 260. I throttled back but the airspeed indicator failed to respond. To my horror I knew the thing was out of action. What sort of landing would I make? Scared stiff, I came in to land, and to my surprise everything was all right. The engineer officer put my aeroplane unserviceable. Later that day I had the pleasure of being flown back to my base in a Blenheim piloted by the squadron-leader who had been controlling our efforts to protect the convoy.

My next trip was a scramble to intercept some Hun machines on recco off Dungeness. I was No. 3 in the front section of six aircraft or, as we called it, a "flight." We stooged around for about half an hour on various courses given us by the controller. Suddenly a large form loomed up in front of us. We had caught our prey. The Hun immediately put his nose down and dived for the sea about 5,000 feet below, at the same time releasing his bombs, no doubt by the jettison button, for they went down in a large mass, hitting the sea in almost the same form as they left the aircraft. In the meantime we had been ordered into "line astern" for the attack. This attack was the only perfect attack, as per written instructions, made by a section in which I have been flying. The section-leader went in, attacked and broke away, No. 2 likewise and then myself. I got in a good burst, with considerable opposition from the rear gunner and all manner of objects thrown from the enemy, such as pieces of wire, rather like old netting from old chicken-runs and small missiles of varying shapes and sizes. Having dodged the objects thrown I found myself going much too fast, and almost collided with the tail of the enemy aircraft, which I recognised as a DO. 17. I did a very split break away, terrified the front gunner would get me as I overshot. Next I knew there was something wrong with my aeroplane, but owing to the thick mist I could see nothing below or above. I took command of myself and stuck my head in the cockpit to sort things out on the blind flying panel. After what seemed minutes to me I suddenly realised that my aeroplane was upside down. I pulled the stick hard back and completed the bottom half of my loop. As I got nearly round to my correct position I saw the water very close. It's a job to describe my feelings at that moment. The nearest I can get is to say I was dumbfounded. Instinctively I rammed the throttle full open and pulled back harder on the stick. Fortunately I just missed the water. I climbed up again and very carefully flew back to my base, feeling completely lacking in physical strength. I realised afterwards the obvious thing to have done was to have just rolled the aircraft into the correct right side up; also that it would be good policy to shut the throttle before attacking and open it if dropping out of range rather than overshoot.

During our waiting periods on the ground the pilots use a room in the Dispersal. There we all talk, play games, write letters to our relatives, read new orders and discuss generally our tactics against the crafty Hun. By this method we sort out the best way to attack various types of Hun aircraft. The Intelligence Officer is often present and picks up lots of useful information, which the pilots have omitted to tell him in the excited statement given him on landing. One Intelligence Officer in a squadron I was with was very cunning. On landing he only wanted to know the number of enemy aircraft destroyed or damaged and nothing further. Later in the day, however, he would come round and get into general conversation with one, by which time the pilot concerned would have been able to think about his last engagement and have a really clear view of what took place, the type of formation adopted by the Huns, the squadron reaction, and generally learn precisely the type of fight that took place. This method was favoured by the pilots, for it enabled them to fill in a combat report very much more accurately than would have otherwise been possible.

We had pictures hanging around the Dispersal of various types: glorious women in the scantiest of clothing, also silhouettes of German aircraft for our study, showing gun positions and range of fire, which means how many degrees the gunner can move his guns to get at attacking fighters. In addition we had pictures of don'ts and do's issued by Fighter Command. These pictures showed a pilot diving on his girl friend's house, giving the neighbourhood a thrill, but entirely omitting to notice a pylon close to the house. This he unfortunately hit after one of his low dives. Such pictures are far better than tons of bumf, for they show the real thing, thus impressing on every person the danger of such tricks. I frequently used to go out and talk to the crew of my aeroplane. This I found to be a very good policy, for by so doing one gets to know the capabilities of the men and it also gives them an interest and something to work for. A little talk with the fitter about the engine and its performance helps him quite a lot to locate little troubles without putting the aircraft unserviceable. The rigger also likes to know how the aeroplane flies and if he can improve its qualities. Every pilot likes his flying kit in a certain position in the cockpit, so if you go along and tell the crew just how you like your helmet positioned and gloves in a definite place, parachute either in the pilot's seat with the straps in easily-get-at-able places, or on the tail plane so that the fitter can be starting the engine whilst the pilot is getting his parachute on. Attention to small details is a very considerable help to the pilot in getting off the ground quickly. If we were more than four minutes getting the whole squadron into the air the C.O. wanted to know what was wrong. One thing that would have been very impressive, if the public could have seen it, I'll endeavour to describe. The squadron is at readiness, the crews are by the aircraft and pilots in the Dispersal Hut. The telephone rings, every pilot springs to his feet, ready to dash to his aeroplane. Betty, the driver of our Humber brake, starts the engine, ready to take pilots who have a long way to go round to their aircraft. "It's a lady to speak to Pilot-Officer Hotstuff about a date he didn't keep." Everybody relaxes again and Pilot-Officer "Peg-leg" puts on another Bing Crosby record, to everybody's delight. Again the phone rings. Up we all get again and I pop a piece of chewing-gum into my mouth. Chewing-gum is a great help when flying, I think; it keeps the saliva up and prevents a dry feeling in the back of one's throat. This time it's the waiter from the sergeant's mess, who wants to know how many late dinners to save. Betty, a plump little thing with large brown eyes and semi-bleached hair, again switches off her engine as the pilots relax. We start to play table tennis. On goes "The Pessimistic Character with the Crab-apple Face" for the benefit of one flight-sergeant who has just reported three unserviceable aircraft and doesn't know when they will be ready to fly again. A queer guy, we all think, but it makes no difference what we think. Amidst the ping-pong of the table tennis and the gramophone, with an officer and sergeant jittering on the floor, the phone rings again. "Squadron take off, patrol Dover-Dungeness 20,000 feet." The telephone operator yells to the nearest crew through the window, "Start up." In a few seconds every engine bursts into life. Betty had departed with her load of pilots. She's a good driver and knows where to stop for each pilot. We are all in our cockpits and straps done up. The fitter's last words as we taxi out are, "The oxygen is on, Sarge, and best o' luck." We are on the aerodrome, sorting ourselves out into prearranged sections of three. We take off six at a time right across the aerodrome. No sooner have the first flight got half-way across the aerodrome than the second flight opens up. We are off on an interception of German raiders coming to bomb some shipping in Dover Harbour. The controller tells the C.O. to go flat out, and he does. We get to the coast and see nothing, having climbed all the way. We can't get to 20,000 feet because it would be above the cloud. No German could bomb a convoy from above the cloud. We, that is my section, are ordered to climb through the cloud to see what's about up there and report to the C.O., who was patrolling under the cloud, ready to pounce on any enemy aircraft that would come down through the cloud in search of the convoy. My section consisted of four aircraft. We batt up through about 3,000 feet of thick cloud as quickly as possible. Just as we come through the cloud we rush into lovely sunshine. It's a wonderful sight to see the sun shining on the billowy clouds below, though we didn't on this occasion have time to enjoy it, for as we got about 500 feet above the cloud and had time to look around, Hun dive-bombers, they were JU. 87's, were diving through the cloud to attack the ships. We wheeled to starboard after them and at the same time got jumped by a number of ME. 109's from above. The fourth man of the section was considerably more crafty than the other three of us. He climbed farther up before turning to dive on the bombers. In so doing he saw the escort fighters whizz past him to attack us. I was on the outside of our turn to attack; consequently it will be appreciated I had quite a lot farther to go than my leader and his No. 2. Next I knew was that four 109's were diving at me. I rolled my aeroplane on to its back and went straight down. Two of the 109's followed me. This is where our No. 4, crafty Sgt. Hamy, saved the situation, for he dived on the 109's. They were scared stiff, because they didn't know how many Spitfires were coming down on them from behind. The result of Hamy's strategy was well repaid, for the bombers were either shot down or so badly disorganised that the bombs were dropped into the water, not one of the ships being touched. The squadron claimed about six JU. 87's destroyed, and the Hurricanes arriving to guard the ships against further attacks, we returned to our base. A very happy squadron, all listening to some dance music by one of the famous bands on the way back. This was possible by tuning the set from the cockpit, of course against regulations, though we could hear the controller if he called and simply tuned in to him again.

Aerial attacks on convoys were becoming the rule, consequently we had the job of patrolling convoys fairly regularly. It's a binding job while there is nothing doing, just stooging up and down and getting more fed-up each run. Readiness would be at 4 o'clock in the morning. Some of the pilots had slept at Dispersal and others would roll up in the brake looking tired, for hours were long in those days, usually from daybreak to dusk. The kit would be put in our respective aeroplanes by the crew, who had already revved the engine to full power and checked everything and reported to the flight-sergeant. The telephone rings: Would the Senior Officer speak to the Controller. He would be told there was convoy off Beachy Head and we had to supply one section to fly over it until 9 a.m., when the Hurricane squadron from the same aerodrome would take over from us. Off went the first section of three aircraft. I usually was in the first section and stooged along as economically as possible once we reached the convoy. We would fly over it first to let them see who we were, then proceed to introduce ourselves to each ship in turn. We would fly very low over and round the ships as they went on their zigzag courses. The crews would wave all manner of queer things to us. I remember on one particular occasion, from a deckhouse of a small ship emerged a very fat man in a pair of trousers and vest only. He put the bucket he was carrying on the end of a broom and started juggling. Others waved caps, shirts and any old thing they could get hold of. I used to think, "Poor devils down there, they must have a rotten life, what with torpedoes and bombs it can't be pleasant." Apparently they enjoyed the security, for each convoy would greet us in a similar way. We'd stooge about down there for an hour and then another three would take over from us. By about noon the food ships would be nearing Dover. Instead of having one section on patrol there would be probably three or four squadrons near the ships. The Goering effort would send over ME. 109's first to try and split up the escort fighters, then about ten minutes after would come the bombers. Some of the best dog-fights I have been in would develop in a few seconds. I would say aloud to myself, "Here the stupid bastards come; why the bloody hell didn't they do it in the early morning, not wait till midday?" No time to think any more, for aeroplanes would be whizzing round in small circles and tracer bullets flying in all directions. Suddenly you saw an aeroplane burst into flames and go down like a stone. "Hope it's a 109," would flash through one's mind. Waugh! nearly hit a Hurricane, blast his eyes; he's after the same Hun as me; let him get on with it, plenty more for me. A nice juicy bomber about to attack an isolated ship, down I go after him. I'm not the only one to have noticed it, another Spit. follows me down. We both hesitate before attacking. Never seen a German bomber like that before, better make sure it is a Hun. I break away to have a look at the markings. Sure enough, the black crosses were there. I recognise the machine as a French Chance-Vaught bomber. We shoot it down into the sea between us. The other pilot turned out to be my Flight Commander. Another bit of information for the Intelligence Officer. The Huns are using French machines they have captured. Suddenly all is quiet. The battle is over. I decide to have a look round the ships before going home. They scattered and one is down at the stern. I wonder if any of the crew are hurt; several small boats are alongside, so I depart thinking that the best possible is being done for the crew and the ship. On the way home I think of the scrap we have just had. The result seems to be very poor compared with the number of fighters and bombers sent over to sink our ships. I am last back and am getting quite a reputation for being the last home. My crew want to know what has happened. I delay a few moments and give them a brief outline. They appreciate that and set to work to get my plane ready in the shortest possible time. I join the other pilots and we have our customary excited chat about our last battle. The Flight Commander is talking to the Intelligence Officer about his attack on the French machine. I am able to assist him and make it known that I was with him when he attacked. We retire to the Dispersal Hut for refreshment. Our Intelligence Officer has ordered coffee to be sent up for us on our return. "Good old

Wallie" comes simultaneously from all the pilots. The flight-sergeant comes in to say all aircraft are refuelled and ready to take the air again. We're off! To relieve the Hurricanes on the convoy again. All is quiet this time, so we return after our hour's patrol without incident.

The Huns are now beginning to blitz our forward bases and we have several clashes with the enemy farther inland. Then the Battle of Britain really started. I'll never forget the first time I saw the Germans coming to attack our inland aerodromes. We were flying at about 15,000 feet when we saw the Huns. They looked rather like a swarm of bees in flight. One solid mass surrounded by whirling aeroplanes. Bombers in the middle, hordes of fighters all round them; some very close and others spread out over the sky. I felt very lonely and very much afraid at first. There seemed to be only twelve of us against all that number. Of course there were plenty of other squadrons near but I couldn't see them at the time. We carried on and went straight through them head-on. It was a strange experience as the large black bombers swept over our heads and underneath us in their efforts to dodge head-on collisions. To be quite frank, I really don't know how we all got away without hitting them. We got the order to turn and every man for himself. Looking back as we turned, one could see the result of our first encounter with the large formation of Huns. They split up and we took advantage of the position. The fighters seemed to be so shocked at the bombers' split they didn't get cracking at it for a bit. By this time dog-fights were developing all over the sky. I imagine the result would be similar if wasps and bees were mixed in a fight. As soon as I saw them split I forgot my fright and got cracking with my aeroplane as a fighting machine. I selected a big long Flying Pencil as a target. He dropped his bombs and turned for home. I chased him, attacked several times and eventually got it down in a field near the coast. I was again on top of the world, for it was my first confirmed victory, and all alone too. I circled over the enemy and took my map from the holder to mark the spot where he crashed. I then proceeded to beat the sod up. As I came down in my first dive I saw the pilot climb out, and as I pulled up I looked back at the big black object on its belly in the field, its flying finished and the crew prisoners. One was injured, for I could see the remainder of the crew carrying him away from the aeroplane. I dived again; this time the pilot, who seemed little interested in the other crew, shook his fist at me and threw his "Mae West" viciously on the ground. I saw a farmer walking across to the machine with a 12-bore sporting gun under his right arm. I left the scene and returned to my base once again, this time with something really worth telling Wallie. On my way back I could hear the Controller telling all A/C to be extremely careful when landing. When I got to the base and saw the condition of the flying field, I thought the Controller a perfect optimist, for I couldn't see a place at first in which to land, there were so many bomb craters. However, I studied the position and decided to land on one runway with a large crater about two-thirds of the way down it. I juggled the aircraft in safely, feeling greatly relieved. I had hardly enough petrol to go farther. To my amazement there was a Spitfire in the crater on the runway. It was our Jitterbug fan, Mr. "Pegleg." His windscreen had stopped a direct hit, it had also shattered some of the perspex screen and cut his face. He couldn't see where he was going after landing, so finished in the crater. It was quite a difficult task to keep going with an airfield filled with craters. There were several delayed-action bombs which would burst at any old time. I often wondered what would happen if one burst when we were taxi-ing with the wing right over the little mound which signified there was a bomb, unexploded, below. However, we carried on the great fight, though our take-off time was considerably lengthened, as may well be imagined. I remember on one very hot day the squadron was off to intercept the masses of German aircraft at about noon. One of our pilots, who was returning from forty-eight hours' rest, reached the gate as the "tannoy" announced that a raid was imminent and would all available pilots please take any aircraft they could find up to help defend the aerodrome. I should explain the Tannoy System is a series of loud speakers all over the aerodrome, operated by the controller or Commanding Officer of the station. Sergeant Chany nipped smartly over the hedge, grabbed a "Mae West," parachute, and helmet, and took my aeroplane, which had been unserviceable when we went off some three-quarter hours previously. I was flying his aeroplane. He took off, intercepted a Hun bomber near our base, shot it down, and returned to the aerodrome for more ammunition. All in the space of twenty minutes. Incidentally his leave was not up until 1 o'clock that day. When we returned the Huns had dropped a large bomb exactly where my aeroplane had stood before Chany took it. We all took a very good view of our Dead Eye Dick pilot after that. Just outside the aerodrome lay a Dornier 17 in a field on its belly. After we were released that night, which was about 11 p.m., we strode over to look at our enemy's aircraft. We got some fitters to cut out the large black cross for us and hung it in the mess. There it acted as a fire-screen for a long time. The blitzing of the aerodromes had ceased in large scale and the Hun seemed to be trying to get to London. As we intercepted the raiders I would be thinking of a girl friend who was probably at that moment hurrying to a shelter from the office in which she is employed. I catch a glimpse of a few crafty sods breaking up, turning for home, and then a few seconds later about-turning and on again towards London. It was my ambition to fire at one of these types and explode his bombs for him. One day I almost succeeded in doing it. I got underneath and to the sun side of a JU. 88. I then throttled back and waited for the raider to get just a little ahead so I could aim accurately at him. However, my luck was out, for just as I pressed the tit to fire the guns, he dropped the load of bombs and dashed for home. I was furious, so proceeded to get him down anyway. This I managed to do successfully, though whilst sitting too close behind after using all my ammunition, having put the rear gunner and both engines out of action, one of the gunners suddenly opened fire at me. He was a good shot too. One of his bloody bullets went through my perspex windscreen, hit the side of my helmet and went out of the back. Another single bullet entered my port wing and made everything inside unserviceable. Another lesson learnt. Never wait in range for your victim to crash – he may have a crafty one up his sleeve. By this time I was becoming very tired and could keep plenty of spirit if I was flying, but as soon as I came down I was yellow of being bombed. We had a dose of bombing one evening about 6.15 p.m. We had just landed, six of us, and were having our oxygen bottles charged and refuelling the aeroplanes. Everybody was brassed-off. We had been up about four times and seen nothing that day. We had the wireless on in the Dispersal and were listening to the news. After which one of our sergeants was going to broadcast. He had shot down five 109's in a day and was to tell the listeners his experiences. The phone rang, "Can you take off?" We couldn't. Our machines were not ready. "Then get to a shelter quickly," was the reply. We took a very dim view, but had no time to argue, for as we looked out of the door an airman said to me, "Look at all those Blenheims, Sarge." I ordered him into the shelter for they were enemy bombers. We took our portable radio with us to the shelter. Whilst we were being bombed Sergeant Chany was talking to the listening millions in his usual calm way. Every one of us decided we would much rather fly with hundreds of Huns around us than be bombed on the ground. When bombs start to fall I always have a feeling of exasperation. I suppose its because one is so helpless on the ground.

I shall never forget my first night operational trip. We had a section of three at a forward base. One fully operational night pilot was staying. I volunteered to stay, and we wanted another. Mr. "Pegleg" also volunteered. The Commanding Officer took a poor view, for I had done one night-landing in a Spitfire and Mr. "Pegleg" two landings. We assured the Commanding Officer that we could cope and he reluctantly let us stay: everybody else had stayed and never been sent off. It's a piece of cake, we thought. I went to sleep in my clothes and "Mae West" and my two companions went for a walk. Suddenly the phone rang. I jumped up and stumbled over beds and what not to get to it. We were ordered off. What a blow! I dashed out on to the aerodrome and yelled for the other two. They were some distance away but heard me. We started up and took off straight from Dispersal. We were sent miles out into the Channel on the track of several raiders. After seeing nothing for about an hour we were completely browned-off. I had never been up for so long at night, the cloud was getting lower and lower and a thick fog was creeping up. "Pegleg" and I hung like leeches to our leader. The long-waited order to return to inland base at long last came through. We flew back on the course given. Our leader called us up and said, "If it doesn't clear, boys, it'll be baling-out by numbers." "To hell with that," I said. Eventually, as we got nearly to our base, the thick mist suddenly cleared. We landed in the order of three, two, one. On reaching the Dispersal we were all congratulated by one of our officers who had been on the flare path, giving us the signal to land. The Commanding Officer and our Wallie, the Intelligence Officer, then rolled up. Whilst we were talking to the Commanding Officer, Wallie discreetly poured out three mugs of beer for us. "Good old Wallie," was the unanimous reply. We went to bed that night feeling quite a lot better than we felt on taking off in the dark.

I have one more confirmed victory which is well worth mentioning. It was towards the end of the Battle of Britain. We had not long landed from another trip. My aeroplane was unserviceable, for one of the guns had jammed on the previous trip. There was not another plane for me, and the armourers were busy when the order to take off was given. Owing to the distance that aircraft have to be dispersed, I was in the habit of riding my bike to my aeroplane. I dashed down to see if there was a possibility of getting up with one gun out of action. I spoke to the armourer about it and he said, "I only want a new barrel, Sarge, and you can go." I sent him for one on my bike. Unfortunately he gave two or three terrific pushes on the pedals and the chain broke. He and bike were all mixed up in a heap on the grass. A good type, he raced off on foot and returned in somebody's car. By this time the squadron was taking off. "Get strapped in, Sarge," was his comment as he came running up. I did as I was bid, thinking him an optimist. But I was wrong, for by the time I was fixed he said, "O.K., off you go." It took just two minutes to fit. I chased after the squadron, and eventually caught them up, just in time to intercept some HE. 111's almost over the aerodrome. We came up behind them this time and couldn't get anywhere near for ack-ack fire. The Commanding Officer asked them to cease fire, which they did, but the bombers were getting mighty close to Tilbury Docks. We went in to attack from straight behind. This is a dangerous practice when there are a number of bombers together because the fire from the rear gunners is terrific. However, we thought the risk was worth it. Four of us went in to attack whilst the others remained behind to ward off any attacking 109's. The four of us that went in first did so in line abreast to confuse the gunners. The result was good. The bombers split up, jettisoned their bombs. The rest of the squadron came in and we had a party that day. I think nearly everybody got something that day and it all happened over the aerodrome where the troops should have been in shelters. But not they, when the squadron was in action above them. I remember one Hun just breaking up and coming down in flames very close to the aerodrome under the withering fire of one of the Flight Commanders. I got one too. It was one of the run-away ones. I did my usual attacks and stopped his port engine. The other wouldn't seem to stop – it only slowed up and the under-carriage came hanging down in a limp fashion. That was the best indication I got that he was done for. We were well above cloud at the time I made my attack. I was afraid I would lose my victim when he came down. The cloud was cumulous and he decided to come down through a hole. This pleased me, as I could keep an eye on him. One has plenty of time to think when just waiting for an aeroplane to glide down. I kept at a safe distance and tried to picture myself in their shoes. Prisoners, I thought; they'll probably be much happier here in prison than fighting a war. I decided it would be the best place for them anyway. I thought of the gunner and wondered if he was dead. I learned after he was. We got lower and lower. I saw an aerodrome below. The Hun turned and I thought he was going to crash in a wood. But he used his crippled engine and just got over the wood, and crashed on the aerodrome. I went down and beat him up, of course. I hadn't a single bullet left, and wouldn't have used it if I had. I spent the last 1,000 feet dodging ground-defence fire. The blighters on the aerodrome opened fire at the Hun but missed him and nearly shot two or three of us, for several Spitfires and Hurricanes had gathered to see the crash. I didn't land but thought I would dash back with the news to my base, because I felt sure some of the other pilots would say they shot the Hun down. I was rewarded for my trouble, because I got the victory confirmed. Incidentally one of our pilots had his engine put out of action by the first lot of ack-ack fire. He landed safely in a field near one of the batteries. I'll leave you to guess what he said to them.

After the Battle of Britain we had the fighter menace to contend with. Higher and higher we had to go, in order to get top sides of the Hun. It's a rather lonely feeling to be very high in the sky with more worries to contend with. Patrol at 30,000 was the common order. It is very cold up there and the windscreen and hood freeze up at the slightest suspicion of moisture. We would run into batches of 109's at various heights. We would either jump them or them us. Dog-fights at fantastic speeds would develop, and in these it was the best pilot who won the day. When stooging along, breathing only oxygen, and not being able to see much owing to a frosty hood, I always felt that he was in the worst position, and had to fly an aeroplane that was considerably more troublesome at those heights than ours. It was just a battle of wits, with little result. I got brassed with this continued high flying, but one gets used to it after a time. I remember on one occasion, four of us got to about seven miles up and chased nine 109's in large circles to the coast, leaving beautiful plumes behind us all the way. The plumes must have been unusual, for in the daily papers next day there were photographs of our trails. I'm sure if the public who looked at them had realised that it took about an hour to thaw our hands when we got down, they would have been sorry such beautiful photos had been taken. We kept going through the winter when weather permitted and then started our spring offensive. Ring twitch was common among the pilots, but not one admitted it. I know I felt far worse when we talked about our next job on the ground than when actually engaged in the operation. Unfortunately I got the wrong end of a 109 one day. He was a very crafty sod, and what is more had bags of guts. He attacked me all on his own, when I was flying with two squadrons. I didn't see him at all. My mirror and hood were frozen. All of a sudden I heard over the radio, "Look out." I hadn't time. He had fired as the words of warning were spoken. He got me but not all of me. I was out of action for some months after crashing, luckily on an aerodrome. The more I think of the life of a fighter-pilot, the more I think a considerable amount of luck plays a big part. That Hun had every advantage, and had he been a good shot or not got scared at the last moment, I should not be writing this story. I'm only waiting to get another crack at the Hun, and when I do, I hope it's a nice fat juicy bomber all to myself. I consider the loss of one German bomber worth two fighters for several reasons. It takes longer to build them, costs more money, entails more labour, and we get at the minimum three of their airmen at one go – a point well worth remembering.

Editor's Note

Claude was posted as missing over Holland shortly after he finished these lines, but not before realising his dream of "having another crack," for he finished off two 109's before he himself "bought it."

EPILOGUE

WELL, that's that. That's how the average fighter-pilot lives in war-time.

The squadron is all split up now, in fact none of the authors are with it any longer.

The old squadron knows us not.

When the Battle of Britain was won and the R.A.F. took the offensive, we did our fair share, mostly over a lot of sea. It was great fun and varied from machine-gunning aerodromes and goods trains to fighter sweeps at 30,000 feet. The suspense before an offensive is the worst of it. When we set course and get down to the job, it's good sport, but the bit I like best is beating up the aerodrome on the return. It is amazing how quickly those Germans can run when they have eight machine-guns shooting at them; One day we shot hell out of an aerodrome and smashed about thirteen JU. 88's. I saw men who were working on them falling right and left and I felt no pity. I might have been shooting at an air-to-ground target for all the emotion I felt.

Perhaps after reading our stories, you may think we're a callous bunch because of the light-hearted way in which we treat life and death. I can assure you, however, that this is not so. There is a considerable feeling of camaraderie among all the fighter squadrons in the R.A.F. Yet when a chap doesn't come back, we don't grieve over him. If we did that we'd go completely nuts in no time. We just think that he's been posted to another squadron in a hurry and hasn't had time to say *au revoir*. Sometimes if you lose a very close friend it affects you badly, but not for long. After all, it might just as easily have been yourself, and you wouldn't want any one to mourn over you. Quite a number of chaps keep a "kitty" in the bar at a station, so that when they bite it, the other fellows can have a last round of drinks on them. That's the only way to get along in our job.

I'd just like to mention a few things about our ground crews. I don't think people outside the R.A.F. realise how dependent we are on our fitters, riggers, armourers, wireless operators, etc., for our ultimate success. These lads, many of them straight from civil life, go to it in a manner which is unbelievable to those outside the service. In all sorts of weather you'll find them working on your machine, checking and rechecking, as keen as mustard on their jobs. I'm sure that in the good old blitz days, the ground crews used to get more kick out of a Hun downed than did the pilots. They'd sometimes go completely nuts, throwing cartwheels and yelling their heads off if the bag was good. They're a fine set of chaps and I take my hat off to them.

Since these stories were written we've had quite a bit to do with the Bomber boys. We used to think of the Bomber boys as the hot-air merchants who spent their time in trying to answer the maiden's prayer. But since I've seen them at work, I have nothing but admiration for them. The way they go through the most intense flak, at the same time bombing and keeping perfect formation, amazes me. We took some over on some of those daylight Brest shows where, as you know, the flak takes a lot of beating anywhere in the world. Yet they stuck together as if they were flying over on an Empire Air Day exhibition. Flak was everywhere, and we twisted and turned to avoid it, but those Bomber boys just grinned and bore it.

In exactly the same way, Coastal Command bomb enemy convoys, flying through an absolute hail of sudden death. Sometimes we go along and beat up convoys with cannon-fire, which is very effective, but we don't just fly through the stuff like these twin-fan merchants. They are a grand crowd of chaps and chockful of guts.

Well, I think that's about all I've got to say. I hope that these stories of combat and life in a fighter squadron have given you an insight into the character of the lads who protect our beloved country. They're all very much of a type you know, with very little fundamental differences between any of them. And another thing: just because a man with R.A.F. wings up has not got a gong stuck underneath them, don't think that he's not a hero. I could tell you some amazing stories, mostly unofficial ones, about what some of these hare-brained lads have done, without being able to report it to official circles. If they had done so, they would probably be given a V.C. whilst awaiting their court martial. And most of the work of the R.A.F. is done by that large percentage of pilots who have received no recognition other than the respect in a fellow-citizen's eyes when he spies those silver wings.

I think I'd better shut up now. But don't forget that we're all with you, and that we're simply longing for the day when they try an invasion. Then we'll give them another taste of our mettle, and the Fighter-Pilot will come into his own again.

SLANG

A.T.S.—Advanced Training School.

A/C.—Aircraft (abbreviation for).

Bind (To).—To grumble.

Binders.—People who are always grumbling or people who are just plain bores.

Bin.—He's bin (or he's had it) means he's finished – frequently used to indicate that the individual is killed.

Blood Wagon.—Ambulance.

Booze-wine.—Drink – usually beer.

Brassed-off.—Fed-up.

Browned-off.—Fed-up but usually to a lesser degree than brassed-off.

Brolly.—Parachute.

Brown Job.—Soldier or Army Officer.

Blacked-out.—A physical condition which occurs when the pilot has been subjected to a given degree of centrifugal force in tight turns and pulling out of a dive. The effect is that the blood drains from the head, resulting in loss of sight. If the force applied becomes very much greater the pilot loses consciousness.

Beat-up.—Diving at an object or person with the object of frightening them and quite often yourself also. Also used to indicate "painting a place red."

Bogle.—Women. See also Dames and Broads.

Chocks.—Blocks of wood put in front and/or behind the wheels of an aircraft to stop it moving.

Clock.—Instrument dial, usually applied to the airspeed indicator, e.g., "I was off the clock" – I was travelling faster than the speeds indicated on the dial of the instrument.

Cotton-wool.—Cloud.

To have a Crack at.—To have a go at or shot at a thing.

Creepers.—Boot-lickers.

Dames and Broads.—Women.

Deck.—The ground or aerodrome.

Do's.—A picnic, party or engagement with the enemy. (Aerial combat. A Sweep or other excitement.)

Double Top.—A good shot. (From double 20 at darts.)

The Drink.—The sea.

E/A.—Enemy aircraft.

E.F.T.S.—Elementary Flying Training School.

Erks.—Airmen below rank of corporal.

Fanny Adams.—Nothing or no one: e.g., I saw Fanny Adams – I saw nothing.

Flap.—To be in a Flap – to be all of a dooda – to get all excited about nothing. Usually associated with doing things in a hurry.

Forced Lob.—Forced landing.

F.T.—Flying Training School.

Grappling Hooks.—Making a big effort, e.g., we threw out the grappling hooks and reached for height – we climbed at maximum speed.

12G.—is the mathematical symbol for Gravity. When used in this sense it is the degree of centrifugal force exerted on the body in a tight turn or when pulling sharply out of a dive – see also *Blacked-out* – 12G is an exaggeration, the normal would be 4 to 7G.

Goner.—Finished, dead.

Grease Monkeys.—Mechanics.

To go for a Burton.—To come a cropper.

You've/he's had it.—Is a strange way of expressing the fact that you've had your cake and eaten it, so no more for you/him.

Harness.—Straps to hold you in the aircraft seat.

Heavy stuff.—Heavy anti-aircraft fire.

Hurribirds.—Hurricanes.

Head in the office.—The office refers to the cockpit.

I.T.W.—Initial Training Wing.

Jim Crow.—A machine on a reconnaissance flight.

Kites or Kytes.—Aeroplanes.

Natter.—A chat – if applied to someone else it is sometimes used in the sense that they are chattering a lot of nonsense.

To Nabble.—To catch or get.

O.T. U.—Operational Training Unit.

Ops.—Operations. The organisation which controls the aircraft from the ground.

Pancake landing.—Dropping the machine, rather than flying it, on to the ground.

To Park an Aeroplane.—To leave it or dump it. Sometimes to crash land.

Peelow.—Pilot. (From the French pronunciation.)

To change Pitch.—Referring to variable pitch propeller.

Putting on the horses.—Giving more throttle to increase speed.

Plonk it down.—To land, usually a forced landing.

Poking Charlie.—Making fun of some one or thing.

Ring Twitch.—An odd feeling one gets in anticipating danger; a mixture of fear and excitement.

Scramble.—Take off in a hurry.

Squirt.—To shoot at.

Sticking to one's compass.—Flying on a compass course in bad weather.

Stooge.—A fellow who does all the dirty jobs or running about.

Stooge Patrol.—A patrol on which one has or does not expect to see the enemy.

Stooging along.—Going along without taking much notice of anything.

Tail-end Charlie.—The last man in the squadron or line of A/C.

Tannoy.—A means of broadcasting messages all over a station by loudspeakers. (The system is made by Tannoy Products Ltd.)

Tits.—The Tit is the trigger or fire-button. To play with the Tits implies that one has put in order all the Taps, Controls, etc., in the Cockpit.

Undercart.—Undercarriage – landing wheels.

Upward Charlie.—Upward slow roll.

Vic.—Verbal or written symbol to ensure the correct interpretation of the letter V: *c.f.* C for Charlie. Frequently used to describe aircraft flying in V formation.

Walking-out.—Baling out.

To Weave.—To fly in a series of shallow turns so that you can see all round you.

To get Weaving.—To crack off or go places.

Weaver.—One who is weaving above other aircraft to act as look-out.

Wog.—A coloured person, usually undesirable (Worthy Oriental Gentleman).